MERLEAU-PONTY: A GUIDE FOR THE PERPLEXED

THE GUIDES FOR THE PERPLEXED SERIES

MERLEAU-PONTY: A GUIDE FOR THE PERPLEXED

ERIC MATTHEWS

continuum

CONTINUUM International Publishing Group
The Tower Building
11 York Road
London SE1 7NX

80 Maiden Lane
Suite 704
New York NY 10038

First published 2006
Reprinted 2007, 2008, 2009, 2010

www.continuumbooks.com

British Library Cataloguing-in-Publication Data
A catalogue record for this book is available from the British Library.

978-0-8264-8532-8 (paperback)

Library of Congress Cataloging-in-Publication Data
Matthews, Eric, 1936–
Merleau-Ponty : a guide for the perplexed / Eric Matthews.
p. cm. – (The guides for the perplexed series)
Includes bibliographical references and index.
ISBN 0–8264–8532–4 (pbk.)
1. Merleau-Ponty, Maurice, 1908–1961.
I. Title. II. Guides for the perplexed.
B2430.M3764M376 2006
194–dc22   2005037797

Typeset by Servis Filmsetting Ltd, Manchester
Printed and bound in Great Britain

CONTENTS

PREFACE

Merleau-Ponty is not an easy author to understand, but he more than repays the effort. The difficulty comes, not from any wilful obscurity, but from the sheer subtlety and complexity of his thought. This book is an attempt to guide readers through that complexity. It works by introducing some of Merleau-Ponty's main themes step by step. Its structure is meant to be something like a staircase: by the time readers reach the top stair, they should have a better grasp than when they first set foot on the bottom stair. What looks like the same theme may appear in more than one chapter, but each time it will be in a different context, which should hopefully add a fresh element to understanding. The only way to read the book, therefore, is linear – from the first page to the last page, not skipping anything in between.

Space does not allow me to cover *all* of Merleau-Ponty's concepts, nor would it be helpful to try to do so. What I have tried to do is to discuss the central core of his thought, in the hope that this will enable readers to explore further for themselves. The Bibliography at the end is meant to help with that exploration. In particular, I have said very little about the developments at the very end of Merleau-Ponty's short life, which were published only after his death. This is because they are necessarily unfinished work, and we cannot know where he would have taken these ideas if he had lived. Better to concentrate on the acknowledged texts published during his lifetime, which anyway contain his most original contribution to philosophy.

Finally, I must express my thanks to Hywel Evans, formerly of Continuum, who first encouraged me to submit a proposal for this book. I must also thank my wife Hellen for her patience with me while I wrote it; and my friend and former student Dr Martin Wylie who shares my enthusiasm for Merleau-Ponty and has contributed more to my thinking than he is aware.

CHAPTER 1

PHENOMENOLOGY

INTRODUCING MERLEAU-PONTY

Maurice Merleau-Ponty (1908–61) is much less well-known, especially in the English-speaking world, than his contemporary and
sometime friend Jean-Paul Sartre. Sartre is known even to many
people who have not studied his philosophy because of his novels,
plays, short stories and essays, and because he was a leading public
figure in French society for many years in the mid-twentieth century.
Merleau-Ponty wrote no novels or plays; and although, like most
French intellectuals, he participated actively in general cultural life,
he for the most part followed a typical French academic career. But
his philosophy is not that of a cloistered professor, of interest only to
other professionals. Many would say that he is at least as important
and relevant a thinker as Sartre, and perhaps more original and profound. Like most philosophers (including Sartre) he went out of
fashion after his death, though many psychologists continued to find
stimulation in his ideas. There are signs now of a revival of interest
in what he has to say about a range of philosophical questions. In
particular, the debate about mind and consciousness seems to have
caught up with him. There is no denying that his often dense prose,
as well as the sheer subtlety of his thoughts, makes him a difficult
philosopher to get to grips with; but I shall try in this book to provide
a guide to at least the main outlines of his thought, in such a way as
to show that it is worth making the effort.

A brief account of his life may help to put him in context. Like
Sartre, he studied philosophy at the École Normale Supérieure
(ENS), one of the most distinguished higher-education institutions
in France, in the late 1920s. It was at the ENS that the two men first

met, though they were not particularly close at that time. Their teachers included some of the best-known French philosophers of the time, such as Léon Brunschvicg and Georges Gurvitch. As a result, Merleau-Ponty was well-grounded in the history of western philosophy, as interpreted by these men, but also in contemporary developments. In particular, he attended Gurvitch's lectures on Husserl's phenomenology, and probably heard Husserl himself lecturing in Paris in 1929 (the significance of this will be explained later).

After graduating from the ENS, Merleau-Ponty taught philosophy for a few years in lycées (secondary schools), did a year's research on perception and then, in 1935, took up a junior post in the ENS which he occupied until the outbreak of the Second World War. While there, he completed a doctoral thesis which was later to become his first book, published in 1942, whose English title is *The Structure of Behaviour*. The main influence on him in writing this book was the 'Gestalt' school of psychologists, who emphasized the organized nature of human experience: our perceptions were not, according to them, broken up into atomistic units called 'sensations', but were structured wholes in which the meaning of individual elements depended on their relation to the whole. Merleau-Ponty, however, thought that the Gestaltists were wrong to think of this as an empirical psychological hypothesis. It was, according to him, a philosophical thesis about the essential nature of human experience. But his interest in Gestalt ideas continued even in his later works.

Other influences on him in the first phase of his thinking in the 1930s were the new French interest in Hegel which developed after the First World War, and (connected with that) the 'western Marxism' which founded itself on the rediscovered early writings of Marx. Merleau-Ponty, like many young French intellectuals, was drawn to the lectures on Hegel's *Phenomenology of Spirit* which were given by a Russian émigré called Alexandre Kojève in Paris in the late 1930s. Kojève's interpretation read Hegel from an essentially Marxist perspective, or, it could equally well be said, treated Marxism as an expression of Hegelianism. This 'Hegelianized' Marxism was similar to that of Marxist thinkers like the Hungarian Georg Lukàcs, whose version of Marxism was far less mechanistic than that of official Communism, and so far more acceptable to idealistic young western left-wingers like Merleau-Ponty. (For further discussion of Merleau-Ponty's Marxism, see Chapter 7).

With the outbreak of war, Merleau-Ponty was called up as an infantry officer, but was demobilized when the French army was defeated by the invading German forces, and went back to teaching philosophy in lycées in Paris. He met Sartre again, and this time became much closer to him, when the two men helped to form a small, and not very effective (by Sartre's own admission), Resistance group called *Socialisme et Liberté* (Socialism and Liberty) which tried to make its own small contribution to opposing the German Occupation of France. The group broke up after a year's existence, but Merleau-Ponty and Sartre remained friends and colleagues. They shared the same general left-wing outlook on politics and society, and in 1945 jointly founded the leading French literary and political periodical *Les Temps modernes* (*Modern Times*). Both were editors and directors of the journal, though Merleau-Ponty wrote most of the editorials (which he did not sign) and took overall control of the magazine's political line. In 1948, Merleau-Ponty and Sartre founded a new socialist political party, non-Communist though not anti-Communist, called the *Rassemblement Démocratique Révolutionnaire* (RDR), whose name means the Revolutionary Democratic Grouping. The party, however, was something of a failure: it did not last very long, and did not attract enough support on the Left to act as a serious rival to the huge French Communist Party (PCF).

In 1945, Merleau-Ponty published what many would regard as his most important book, *Phenomenology of Perception*, which again was originally a doctoral thesis. (We shall return to this work later in the chapter, and in much of the rest of the book, since it considers virtually all of the major themes of his thought.) It was also in 1945 that Merleau-Ponty made the move from teaching philosophy in lycées to university teaching, when he became a Professor of Philosophy at the University of Lyon. In 1949, he moved to become Professor of Psychology and Pedagogy at the Sorbonne, in Paris; and finally, in 1952 he was appointed to a Chair in Philosophy at the Collège de France, also in Paris, a post which he held for the rest of his life.

All this time, he was writing and speaking; about philosophy, of course, but also about a range of other subjects including politics, art, literature and the cinema. In 1947, he published a political work, *Humanism and Terror*, which reveals him struggling to come to terms with the revelations of Soviet repression which were increasingly

3

reaching the West, while holding on to a belief in Marxist socialism. These misgivings about Soviet Communism increased in the next few years, and were one of the primary causes of the quarrel between Sartre and Merleau-Ponty in 1953. (Sartre, in strong disagreement with Merleau-Ponty, continued to hold to the view that support for the Soviet Union was necessary if one were to avoid betraying the French working class, most of whom supported the pro-Soviet French Communist Party.) Merleau-Ponty resigned as editor of *Les Temps modernes*, and thereafter took little active part in politics, though he retained an essentially left-wing stance. His book *Adventures of the Dialectic*, published in 1955, expresses his later attitudes to politics, as well as containing a long attack on Sartre's political position. (The two men were reconciled to some extent before Merleau-Ponty's death.)

In 1948, he gave a series of radio talks on his own approach to philosophy, the text of which has now been published, both in French and English (the title of the English translation is *The World of Perception*). He wrote numerous articles about politics and general cultural topics: some of these were published in book form in his collections *Sense and Non-Sense* and *Signs*. His inaugural lecture at the Collège de France was published, along with other essays, as *In Praise of Philosophy*. And, very importantly, towards the end of his life, he was working on two books, both uncompleted at the time of his death, and published only posthumously, in which his thinking took a distinctive new turn. These books are known in English as *The Prose of the World* and *The Visible and the Invisible*. (For full details of all the works mentioned, and of other works by Merleau-Ponty, see the Bibliography at the end of this book.) On 3 May 1961, at the tragically early age of 53 and (as the uncompleted works show) with much still to say, Merleau-Ponty died of a heart attack.

THE TURN TO PHENOMENOLOGY

Some of the influences on Merleau-Ponty's thinking have been mentioned already: Hegel and a Hegelianized version of Marxism and Gestalt psychology in particular. Other influences came from contemporary French philosophers, such as Henri Bergson and Gabriel Marcel, and from the general tradition of western philosophy, above all Descartes and Kant. But by far the most significant influence on his development was the 'phenomenological' movement initiated by

Edmund Husserl. It has already been mentioned that Merleau-Ponty heard lectures by Georges Gurvitch on phenomenology while he was still a student at the ENS, and that he was probably present at the lecture Husserl himself gave in Paris in 1929. But what really 'converted' him to phenomenology seems to have been his discovery of Husserl's later thought towards the end of the 1930s. In 1939, an article appeared in the journal *Revue internationale de philosophie* on fresh developments in Husserl's thinking at the end of his life (Husserl had died in 1938). When Merleau-Ponty read this article, he was so impressed that he immediately made arrangements to visit the newly established Husserl Archive at the Catholic University of Louvain (now Leuven) in Belgium. A Catholic priest from Louvain, Father von Breda, had managed to rescue Husserl's manuscripts from Nazi Germany, where Husserl had in the last years of his life faced the same persecution as other Jews, and where his work was consequently in danger. In Louvain, Merleau-Ponty made a deep study of these writings, most of which were at that time still unpublished, though some of the most important of them had been published in 1936 as *The Crisis of European Sciences and Transcendental Phenomenology*. His work from then on was deeply marked by his understanding of phenomenology, even though in his posthumously published writings he claimed to repudiate the phenomenological standpoint.

Who was Edmund Husserl, and what did he mean by 'phenomenology'? He was born in 1859 in Moravia (now part of the Czech Republic, then a province of the Austro-Hungarian Empire). He studied mathematics and philosophy in Berlin, Vienna and Halle, and then taught philosophy at Halle, Göttingen and Freiburg, until his retirement in 1929. His greatest philosophical achievement in these years was to found the phenomenological movement, one of the central strands of twentieth-century philosophy. Phenomenology claimed to offer a new beginning in western philosophy, though one that incorporated all that was best in earlier traditions, especially the intellectual revolutions carried out by Descartes and by Kant. Like all living schools of thought, it developed over time, but some elements in phenomenology remained constant through these changes. One is the emphasis on human subjectivity. Knowledge and awareness of the world are always *someone's* knowledge and awareness, as both Descartes and Kant had reminded us. Descartes had argued that all sound conceptions of the world must be grounded in our knowledge of our own existence as thinking beings, or subjects (the Cartesian *cogito*: 'I think, therefore I am'). Kant had stressed similarly that the 'I think' must accompany all our representations – that a representation of things must be a representation *to someone*. Husserl saw the function of phenomenology as that of clarifying the essences of the concepts used in the various forms of our awareness of the world about us, including the natural sciences. In his original formulation of phenomenology, he describes both science, and pre-scientific common sense, as part of what he called the 'natural attitude': we naturally take for granted the objective existence of the things of which we are aware, and seek to know more about them. But if we are to pursue such scientific investigations fruitfully, we need to understand what exactly it is that we are seeking to investigate: what do we *mean* by our talk, in psychology for example, of 'consciousness' or 'perception' or, in physics, by our conceptions of 'matter'? To discover that, Husserl argued, we need to set aside the objectivist assumptions of the natural attitude, and concentrate on our own subjective consciousness of how the things referred to *appear* to us (hence 'phenomenology', from the Greek word 'phenomena', meaning 'appearances'). We must get back 'to the things themselves', forgetting any scientific or other theories about the things in question, and sticking to describing our concrete human experience of them, on which any such theories must, after all, be based. This ranking of concrete experience as more important than abstract theorizing makes phenomenology, as Merleau-Ponty says, part of 'the general effort of modern thought' (Merleau-Ponty 2002: xxiv).

This emphasis on subjectivity might suggest that phenomenology was simply a form of introspective psychology, retreating from the objective world into our 'inner selves'. But that is not how Husserl and his followers saw subjectivity. The 'subjective' is not a separate inner world, but is necessarily related to the world we are conscious of. To make this point, Husserl took over a concept from the nineteenth-century Austrian philosopher Franz Brentano (1837–1917): the concept of the 'intentionality' of consciousness. Brentano had found this term in the writings of mediaeval logicians, and had thought it neatly expressed what distinguished the 'psychic' (mental) from the 'physical'. To say that consciousness is 'intentional' is to say that it is always *directed towards* or *refers to* some object: this can be expressed in the slogan 'consciousness is always consciousness *of* something'. For example, thinking is always thinking *about* or of someone or something; being afraid is always being afraid *of* something; hoping is always hoping *for* something. It is impossible just to think without thinking about an object, or to be afraid without being afraid of something, and so on. The object that we are conscious of can be called the 'intentional' object. There are several interesting things to be said about the intentional objects of consciousness. First, something can be an intentional object without actually existing, and we can say that something is an intentional object without knowing whether it exists or not. For instance, we can be afraid of something which doesn't really exist, as in a child's fear of the bogey-man. And to say that some people are afraid of ghosts implies nothing about whether ghosts really exist or not. This means that to say that something is the intentional object of our consciousness is not the same as saying that it *causes* our consciousness of it, since only things which really exist can be causes. Thus, the relation of our consciousness to its intentional objects is not a causal one, and the study of how intentional objects appear to consciousness (phenomenology) is not the same as the study of the causes of our consciousness of objects (empirical psychology or physiology).

Secondly, we are conscious of an intentional object *under some particular description* and not under others. For instance, I might be thinking about Tony Blair without knowing that he is the current Prime Minister of the United Kingdom. If someone asked me whether I was thinking about the British Prime Minister, I should then reply, 'No, I'm thinking about Tony Blair', and that would be a true statement about my present thoughts, even though, looked at from the outside, to think about Tony Blair in 2005 is to think about the current Prime Minister of the United Kingdom. So we can say what I am thinking about without reference to what is in fact the case. In this sense, the phenomenological study of how things appear to our consciousness is distinct from the study of how things are 'objectively', in the outside world, and can be carried on independently of any such objective study.

Thirdly, the different forms of our consciousness obviously relate to their intentional objects in different ways. To believe in ghosts and to be afraid of ghosts, for instance, have the same intentional object, but they relate to that intentional object differently. A belief in ghosts, as such, is simply the acceptance of a certain proposition ('There are such things as ghosts'). A fear of ghosts, on the other hand, necessarily involves certain kinds of behaviour – shivers down the spine in places which are believed to be haunted, avoidance of such places, and so on. A love of ghosts would also involve behaviour and responses to the experience of ghosts, but behaviour and responses which are of a different kind from those involved in fear. In some individuals' experience, belief in ghosts and fear of ghosts may be inextricably entangled, but it does not follow that belief and fear are *conceptually* indistinguishable. An important part of phenomenology, as the study of how things appear to consciousness, is thus the study of the different ways in which the same things appear to different modes of consciousness, such as thought, perception, fear, love, imagination, and so on. To put it another way, we need to understand, not only what ghosts are or what we mean by 'ghosts', but also what we mean by 'thinking', 'perceiving', 'imagining', 'loving', and how the essence of one of these modes of consciousness differs from that of the others. Indeed, it might be argued that study of the different modes of consciousness of objects and their essential differences must come before study of the essences of what we are conscious of, and much of phenomenological literature is in fact concerned more with the essences of different modes of consciousness than with those of the different objects of consciousness. (Merleau-Ponty's own studies of the phenomenology of perception are a case in point.)

A phenomenology based on the acceptance of the intentionality of consciousness is thus different from an empirical introspective psychology in a number of important ways. First of all, it is not empirical. It is not concerned with what the world is objectively like, which would need empirical data provided by observation and experiment, but with what the objects that we believe ourselves to experience in the world *mean to us*, or with what our belief in them means. We can establish that without the need for empirical data about the outside world (and so a priori), just by reflecting on our own experience. Secondly, it is not introspective. Consciousness, if it is intentional, cannot be studied separately from its objects, which are outside us (even, paradoxically, if they don't exist!). One way in which Husserl differed from Brentano was that Brentano thought of intentional objects as existing 'in' consciousness, whereas Husserl saw that that could not be correct, since it is contrary to what 'intentionality' means. Someone who believes in ghosts does not just believe that the *idea* of ghosts exists (something which could be accepted by the most dedicated sceptic about the supernatural), but that *actual* ghosts exist 'out there', waiting to be encountered on dark nights. What the sceptic doubts, similarly, is that there are such actual ghosts. So to study our consciousness of ghosts (or anything else) is not to look inside our minds to study our ideas of ghosts, but to study what both the believer and the sceptic mean by 'ghosts', what part that concept plays in our shared human experience, as a potential inhabitant of the world outside our minds.

Thirdly, phenomenology is not (scientific) psychology, both because, as has just been said, it is not reliant on empirical data, and also because it is *descriptive* rather than *explanatory*. Scientific psychology (like all sciences) does not only seek to establish the facts about its particular domain, but to give a *causal explanation* of how those facts come to be so: what causes what to happen. For instance, a psychological study of perception would have to try to explain how it comes about that we see things: light reflected from the object seen impinges on our retinas, which in turn causes certain responses in the optic nerve, and so on. But phenomenology is not concerned with such explanations, only with describing what is essential to our perception of such objects – what it means to us to 'perceive' such an object. The answer to such questions certainly has a bearing on empirical psychology (and on other relevant sciences), since it helps in trying to give a scientific explanation of, say, perception to have a clear idea of what it is exactly that one is trying to explain. And Merleau-Ponty thought, as we shall see, that in a sense a knowledge of empirical scientific findings could be relevant to phenomenology. A reading of the psychological literature might suggest, for example, that some of the explanations offered were unsatisfactory, not because they were refuted by empirical observations, but because they were based on confused *philosophical* assumptions. This would then give us a motive to try to undermine these assumptions, and so clarify the concepts used in the explanation, by means of phenomenological analysis. But this, of course, still makes phenomenology a distinct activity from any empirical science.

THE PHENOMENOLOGICAL REDUCTION

We can now understand better a central feature of phenomenological method which was briefly mentioned earlier. To pursue phenomenology as a distinct activity, we need to separate the consideration of 'phenomena', as things which appear to us subjectively, from considering them as things actually existing in the objective world and studied by empirical science. The way to do this, according to Husserl in his early thought, is what he calls the 'phenomenological reduction', which he compares in some respects to Descartes's method of doubt. Descartes had tried to arrive at absolutely certain foundations for knowledge by doubting any beliefs that it was possible to doubt, which included, as he saw it, even our basic confidence in the existence of a world outside our own thoughts. The hope was that eventually he would come to at least one belief that it was completely impossible to doubt, and this would then provide the basis for certainty he was looking for. That foundation was found, in Descartes's eyes, in the existence of our own thoughts, and in our own existence as thinking beings. The 'doubt', of course, was a kind of pretence (or, to put it in more flattering terms, it was 'methodological'): Descartes never *really* doubted that the outside world existed, he just treated the existence of the world *as if* it were doubtful, for the purposes of his method.

In somewhat the same way, though for different purposes, Husserl tried to separate consideration of our experience of objects, just as an experience, from consideration of all questions to do with their actual existence. He proposed that we should, as it were, 'put in brackets' what he called our 'natural attitude'. The 'natural attitude' is the one we adopt most of the time when we are not engaged in phenomenology: it is the attitude both of ordinary common sense and, at a more sophisticated level, of science. We take for granted the existence of the objects we think about and deal with practically, and try to understand how one such object relates to others. We *must* do this if we are to live at all. But in the phenomenological reduction, we 'bracket' these assumptions, because as phenomenologists we are not concerned with the demands of practical living but with a more detached attempt at a purely theoretical understanding of what we mean by certain concepts. Husserl often uses as an alternative to 'bracketing' the Greek word *epoche* (meaning literally 'holding back'): we as it were step back in the reduction from our everyday practical involvement with the world in order to study phenomena *just as* phenomena, without regard to their actual existence. Having done this, we can more effectively consider the 'essences', the distinctive meaning of each concept, without the distraction of questions concerning the existence of things corresponding to that concept. Thus, phenomenology is a 'transcendental' study, one which investigates thoughts just as thoughts, without reference to the objects that these thoughts are about.

There are, however, serious doubts about the validity of this notion of transcendental phenomenology. It seems to be inconsistent with the implications of the very idea of the intentionality of consciousness which Husserl himself had made so central to phenomenology, and to be in serious danger of sliding into philosophical idealism, the view that only thoughts exist, and that what we call the objective world is just a kind of construction out of thoughts. The idea of intentionality implies, as we have seen, that consciousness cannot be considered separately from its intentional objects – that we cannot, for instance, think without thinking *about* something, something which is not part of our consciousness. The thing we think about on any particular occasion need not actually exist, but it does not follow that we could investigate our thoughts about that thing in isolation from all considerations of its existence. To say that it is an intentional object is to say that it *could* exist, and that means independently of our minds. We cannot consider our consciousness, therefore, without thinking of the relation of that consciousness to a world independent of it, so that complete 'bracketing' is impossible. We ourselves, as conscious subjects of experience, cannot think of ourselves in isolation from a world to which our experiences refer – even our imaginary experiences presuppose a world in which the imaginary objects *could* feature. We are not 'transcendental subjects', as Husserl argued, pure subjects of thought who do not exist at any particular time or place, but concrete human beings, living in a particular time and place, and finding meaning in objects by virtue of our actual dealings with them in that time and place.

One of Husserl's greatest students was Martin Heidegger (1889–1976). Heidegger says in his work *Being and Time* (Heidegger 1962) that what he initially found puzzling about phenomenology was that it was supposed to be neither logic nor psychology. That is, it neither studied the a priori laws of logic, which hold whether or not anyone thinks of them, nor the empirical facts about what goes on in real human beings when they think. It is supposed to be a study which combines elements from both logic and psychology: it is about consciousness, but not that of any particular person, just consciousness as such. After meeting Husserl in 1916, Heidegger says, his puzzlement decreased, though only slowly. He came to think that phenomenology was not best seen as a metaphysical theory, like idealism, about what exists or does not exist, but a certain way of thinking. In *Being and Time*, he describes phenomenology as primarily a 'methodological conception' (Heidegger 1962: 50), a way of inquiring into objects, not something to be defined in terms of the kind of objects investigated.

Heidegger also had his own definition of 'phenomenology', based on what he claimed to be the meaning of the Greek words from which the term is derived (*phainomenon* and *logos*). This definition is rather tortuously expressed as 'letting that which shows itself be seen from itself in the very way in which it shows itself from itself' (Heidegger 1962: 58). More simply expressed, it is a return, in Husserl's slogan, 'to the things themselves', the effort to think of the world of our experience without preconceptions – to let the world, or Being, speak for itself. (Heidegger's translators always use a capital 'B' when referring to 'Being' in this sense.) 'Ontology' is the traditional philosophical term for the study of Being as Being, of what it means for anything to be. Heidegger is fundamentally concerned in his philosophy with ontology in this sense, but in *Being and Time* he says that 'the question of the meaning of Being' must be treated phenomenologically (Heidegger 1962: 50).

To treat the meaning of Being phenomenologically is to start from our own experience of Being: but that does not mean to look inside our own minds at our inner experiences, nor to separate (as Husserl tended to do in his early thinking) our consciousness from its objects. Our own Being, Heidegger argued (and in this he was followed by Merleau-Ponty), is Being-in-the-world. (The German term is a single word, *Inderweltsein*: this expresses the unity of the concept, which we have to express in English by the hyphens.) We do not exist apart from the world we experience, but are part of it. We are, however, a peculiar part of the world, by virtue of the fact that we are *conscious* of it. This human mode of Being Heidegger called *Dasein* (the German word for 'existence', which literally means 'being there'). We experience the world, in other words, not as detached subjects or pure reason, but as actual human beings who exist at a particular time and place, and who interact with their surrounding world from that position in space and time. Phenomenology, therefore, must be, not the analysis of some detached pure consciousness, but 'the analytic of *Dasein*', as Heidegger called it: the analysis of how things appear to us in the course of our ordinary human interactions with the world.

In the works which he wrote in the last years of his life, Husserl seems to have recognized the force of Heidegger's criticisms of his early 'transcendental' phenomenology, and to have developed a version of phenomenology which, while retaining as much as possible of his earlier thought, attempted to take account of these objections. Central to this later version is the idea of the *Lebenswelt*, or 'life-world': the starting-point of phenomenology is no longer the act of 'stepping-back' from our ordinary involvement with the world. Instead, we have to accept that, before all theorizing, we are already involved in a world, and that the test of all our theoretical opinions is to be found in that involvement with a world. 'Is it not in the end', Husserl asks, 'our human being, and the life of consciousness belonging to it, . . . which is the place where all problems of living inner being and external exhibition are to be decided?' (Husserl 1970: 114). Science and philosophy are human activities which arise within this life-world, and so are secondary to it. If we are to return to basics, then, the presuppositions which we have to set aside are those derived from scientific and philosophical theorizing. The crisis which Husserl came to see as affecting western civilization as a whole arose, in his view, as soon as the Greeks misguidedly saw the idea of 'objective truth', as sought in the sciences, as required in all knowledge worthy of the name. Rather, Husserl came to think, we should see science and its values as deriving what force they had from their part in a wider human engagement with the world. The task of phenomenology was now to get back to that underlying foundation of ordinary human experience which is the source of science and all other theoretical activities. Husserl still speaks of an *epoche*, but now it is a holding back from all *theoretical* preconceptions, which will make possible 'a complete personal transformation, comparable in the beginning to a religious conversion' (Husserl 1970: 137).

WHAT MERLEAU-PONTY MEANS BY 'PHENOMENOLOGY'

Merleau-Ponty, as was said earlier, was particularly taken by this later, more Heideggerian, form of phenomenology. Like Heidegger, he saw phenomenology as 'a manner or style of thinking' (Merleau-Ponty 2002: viii) rather than a system of philosophy. Furthermore, this manner or style of thinking had been practised, he thought, before Husserl made it explicit as a method for doing philosophy: it can be found, he said, in such thinkers as Hegel, Kierkegaard, Marx, Nietzsche and Freud. All of these philosophers had been suspicious of the western tradition in philosophy, which originated with the Greeks, especially Plato. According to this tradition, the highest human attribute was pure, impersonal reason. We were at our most human when we set aside our merely individual and local perspectives on the world, infected as they are by our emotional and practical needs, and ascend to a more detached, or 'objective', view of things. That is, we needed to give an account of things, not as they appear to us from where we happen to be, but as they really are in themselves: the kind of account which would be given by a being who did not have any particular position in space or time (this is therefore what the modern American philosopher Thomas Nagel calls 'The View from Nowhere').

This 'objectivist' view runs through most of traditional western philosophy, and gave rise eventually to the acceptance in modern western culture of the mathematical natural sciences as providing the most reliable account of what reality is fundamentally like. For it has been recognized since Plato that mathematical propositions are the clearest example of truths of reason: propositions which are impersonally and timelessly true. '2 + 2 = 4', to take the simplest example imaginable of a mathematical proposition, is not true only for me or only for you, not true only in 2005 or only in Ancient Greece, but is simply *true*, whoever utters it and whenever it is uttered. To the extent that empirical sciences like physics and chemistry (and biology, considered as a derivative of physics and chemistry) can express their discoveries in the language of mathematics – as equations, proportions, ratios and so on – they too acquire the impersonality and timelessness of mathematics. Newton's law of gravitation, for example, which expresses the attraction between two bodies in terms of the mathematical relations of their masses and of the distance between them, is, if true, timelessly and impersonally so. Hence Galileo expressed the essence of the scientific revolution of the sixteenth and seventeenth centuries when he said that the book of nature was written in the language of geometry, and could be understood only by those who had mastered that language.

When applied to such things as planetary motion, or the workings of machines, or the effect of chemicals on the functioning of animal bodies, this approach has proved incredibly fruitful. But does it follow that this is the only sensible way to understand everything we want to understand? When we want to understand human behaviour, for instance, must we adopt a similarly impersonal attitude? Must we see human actions as like the motions of machines, to be explained, like them, in terms of physico-chemical laws? Or does the study of human history or society, or of our experience of poetry or art, or of personal relationships, have to be treated as a branch of physics before it can truly be regarded as respectable? Some philosophers, and many scientists, have thought so. The philosophers known as 'eliminative materialists', for example, want to replace our ordinary understanding of human behaviour in terms of feelings, motives, reasons and purposes, which they dismiss as mere 'folk psychology', by a 'completed neuroscience'. Suppose, for instance, that someone enrols for a course in conversational Italian. In ordinary, non-scientific, thinking we might understand this in terms of her reasons for doing so – maybe she wants to get more out of her forthcoming holiday in Italy. But this, according to an eliminative materialist, is a primitive and unsatisfactory way of making sense of her behaviour – rather like the mediaeval way of understanding why the flames of a fire move upwards while a lump of soil falls to the ground: in terms of the natural striving of each type of matter, up or down respectively. Science, for these philosophers, offers us a better way of understanding, both in the case of the movement of flames and in that of human behaviour. In the latter case, a fuller knowledge of the workings of the brain and nervous system would, they claim, enable us to give a properly based explanation of, say, this person's enrolment in the Italian class.

This idea that scientific explanations are always to be preferred to non-scientific is not confined to philosophers such as the eliminative materialists, but is widespread in our culture, because of the enormous prestige which especially the natural sciences enjoy in the modern world. A description of a situation in 'objective' or 'scientific' terms is regarded as more respectable, as coming closer to representing the reality of the situation, than one which uses purely qualitative language. For instance, talking of wavelengths of light is thought to be better than talking of colours, or talking of brain-processes as better than talking of thoughts or feelings. Human beings come to be seen as just one more kind of object in the world, as nothing but members of a particular animal species or type of biological system, the workings of which have in turn to be explained in terms of physico-chemical processes.

The phenomenological manner of thinking, as understood by Merleau-Ponty, would say that this only leads to confusion, because it gets things the wrong way round. The sciences themselves are, he contends (as Husserl had done), human accomplishments, particular forms of human activity engaged in for particular human purposes: there is no reason for thinking that the theoretical way of understanding required by the purposes of science is the only, or the most fundamental, way of understanding the world and ourselves. Science needs to be understood in terms of its basis in direct human experience, so that it cannot supersede that direct experience. The most fundamental way of understanding ourselves cannot be the 'objective' way of science: as a particular type of object in the world to be explained from the outside. This is because we ourselves give meaning to the concepts used in the sciences, including the concept of objectivity itself, as abstractions from our concrete experience of ourselves and of other human beings. To use his example, we can understand geography only because we know what it is to experience a landscape. In that sense, we are what Merleau-Ponty calls 'the absolute source' (2002: ix).

None of this means that scientific ways of describing the world are somehow invalid. They are inescapable if we want, as human beings do for various purposes, to talk about the world from a more universal point of view, in ways which are not the expression of personal feelings. But we can talk in this more universal way only by starting from our personal engagement with the world. Science is empirical, based on human experience, and human experience is always that of particular human beings who engage with the world in the course of *living in* it, rather than *theorizing about* it. We must get back to that lived experience, back 'to the things themselves', if we are even to understand the role which science plays in our lives. Phenomenology, from this point of view, consists in getting back to bedrock, to direct human experience, setting aside any preconceived ideas derived from our scientific theories, or from philosophies which are based on such scientific theories and attempt to give them a metaphysical status.

This stepping back from theoretical preconceptions is obviously a form of what Husserl called *epoche* or the phenomenological reduction. Merleau-Ponty accepts the idea of the reduction, but insists that we must understand this idea correctly. It must not, he argues, be thought of as a total withdrawal from all engagement with the world into some kind of absolute subjectivity, since that is impossible and is anyway inconsistent with other things that Husserl says. Husserl recognizes, for example, that there are *different* subjects, that I am a different subject and have different experiences of the world from you, or him or her. But even to recognize this implies that I cannot be aware of myself as a subject without also being aware of other subjects – 'I' has meaning only if it can be contrasted with 'you' and other personal pronouns. To accept the existence of other subjects as well as oneself is also to accept that there is a world which all these different subjects experience, each from his or her perspective, and which provides the common 'horizon' for all our experiences. Hence, I cannot withdraw totally into my own subjectivity and sever all ties with the world I am conscious of. I am not, as a subject, outside time and space: I am necessarily 'incarnate' or 'embodied' in a certain historical situation (this idea of human subjectivity as necessarily embodied is of crucial importance in Merleau-Ponty's philosophy, as we shall see later). My experiences are experiences of the world, and the world is what gives meaning to the experiences I have. So I can't separate out the world itself from the world as meaningful to me: human being is, in Heidegger's phrase, 'being-in-the-world'.

In view of this, what does the phenomenological reduction amount to? Merleau-Ponty (2002: xv) cites with approval the formulation of Husserl's assistant, Eugen Fink: the reduction consists in an attitude of 'wonder' towards the world. We cannot withdraw totally from the world – a complete reduction, Merleau-Ponty says, is impossible (ibid.). But we can relax the ties which bind us to things in our practical dealings with them, so that the sheer strangeness of the world becomes more apparent. By abandoning, temporarily at least, the theoretical structures which we have built up to make our practical and social life manageable, and getting back to our immediate, pre-theoretical, experience of the world, we can understand better the meanings of those theoretical structures themselves. 'True philosophy', Merleau-Ponty (2002: xxiii) says, 'consists in relearning to look at the world'. Thus, the phenomenological reduction, in his interpretation of it, is a matter of changing our way of seeing the world. When we practise the reduction, we no longer see the world as the comfortable place we have made it by the scientific and other concepts which we have built up, precisely in order to make it easier to handle intellectually and practically. Instead, we must train ourselves to see it as the strange and ambiguous existence we encounter when we do not interpose these concepts between ourselves and objects. It is the opposite of another sense of 'reduction', as when we speak of 'reductionism', the view that one particular set of concepts (those of a science like physics, for example) can capture the whole reality of things. Merleau-Ponty compares it to art: like art, it does not simply represent a pre-existing truth, but forces us to see the world differently, and in that sense creates a new truth.

Phenomenology, seen in this way, is not the study of some purely abstract essences, like Plato's Forms. The 'essences' which phenomenology studies are rather tools in our attempt to understand our own lives in the world (Merleau-Ponty 2002: xvi). To understand the concepts we use is to grasp the role they play in our lives in the world: so, for instance, to grasp the 'essence' of perception phenomenologically is to understand how perception actually functions in our relations with the world around us and with other people. In this sense, 'essence' cannot be separated from 'existence', the understanding of concepts from the understanding of the world the concepts refer to.

Merleau-Ponty contrasts the phenomenological approach to meaning with that of the Vienna Circle, the 'Logical Positivists' who flourished in the 1920s and 1930s, whose views were communicated to the English-speaking philosophical world above all in Ayer's *Language, Truth and Logic* (first published in 1936). The Logical Positivists saw the task of philosophy as that of the logical analysis of the language of science: questions of meaning (the domain of philosophy) were distinguished from questions of fact (the domain of science). 'Meaning', for them, was the meaning of *words*, and could be studied therefore by studying language, in isolation from the facts that words and sentences in language were supposed to represent. The question of *how* language represented reality was neither a question to be resolved by the analysis of language, nor a factual question to be settled by science: so it was an empty or meaningless question. This is, however, the very opposite, Merleau-Ponty contends, of a phenomenological approach. Language gets its meaning from our experience of and involvement with the world: we need to have contact with the world in a *pre-reflective* or unconscious way before we can start to talk about it explicitly in language. So to understand meanings is not primarily to understand what words mean, but what *things* mean – to understand the roots of our language in what Merleau-Ponty calls 'the ante-predicative life of consciousness' (2002: xvii).

There is an interesting comparison to be made here to the way in which Wittgenstein's thought developed, and the influence which that development had on the analytic tradition in philosophy. Wittgenstein started from a position which had much in common with Logical Positivism (though it was not identical with it). In his early work language is presented as offering a straightforward 'picture' of the facts it represents. But as Wittgenstein reflected on this, he came to see that it was too simple: 'picturing' or 'representing' reality itself needed to be understood in different ways in different contexts. Our words (concepts) represent reality by virtue of our *use* of them in different ways, so that their meaning can be grasped only by grasping the variety of ways in which we use them in our lives. Like Merleau-Ponty, the later Wittgenstein rejected the idea of 'language' as an abstract system which relates to another abstract system called 'the world', and focused more on our words and concepts as things we use as part of our ordinary involvement with our environment.

This gives the idea of 'consciousness' and its 'intentionality' a different significance. The 'intentional objects' of consciousness, it has already been said, are always experienced *under a certain description*. This 'description' is naturally identified with a certain form of words: to use the example already given, I could identify the object of my present thought by the words 'Tony Blair' or 'the current (2005) Prime Minister of the United Kingdom'. In a case like this, it is hard to see how one *could* identify the intentional object of thought in any other way. But perhaps that is because we are talking about *thoughts*, and of a relatively intellectual and sophisticated kind. But our experience of the world in this intellectual way is possible only because we have much less intellectual or reflective forms of contact with the world, which have their own sorts of intentional object, of a kind which we may not normally identify explicitly in words. When I am driving my car, I am not normally explicitly saying to myself, 'Now change gear' or, 'Now apply the brakes'. Nevertheless, I do genuinely recognize the need to change gear in certain situations, and this recognition determines how I act. In other words, my consciousness is directed towards 'gear-change', even though I do not explicitly identify that in words as my intentional object. Reflective, verbalized, explicit, consciousness of the world is rooted in such pre-reflective, non-verbal, implicit consciousness, and intentionality applies as much in the former as in the latter case. So a phenomenology of consciousness is not merely a matter of 'linguistic analysis', in the Logical Positivist sense, but an attempt to bring into reflective awareness the whole mode of our 'being-in-the-world' which is involved in the relevant case.

Phenomenology, as Merleau-Ponty sees it, thus combines a form of subjectivism with a form of objectivism. It is subjectivist in that it recognizes that all experience is *someone's* experience, that 'how things appear' means 'how they appear to *a particular 'subject'*. A description of phenomena, that is, of how things appear, must thus necessarily be a description of *subjective experience*. But, since the being of subjects is being-in-the-world, that is, since experience consists in being involved with the world, a description of subjective experience is not a description of something purely 'inner', but of our involvement with a world which exists independently of our experience of it. The world, Merleau-Ponty says, is not something we merely think about, but the place in which we live our lives, the world we act in, have feelings and hopes about, as well as the world we try to know about. Phenomenology, in his sense, is thus a kind of anti-philosophical philosophy. It seeks not to rise above our practical and emotional involvement with the world in order to offer an explanation or justification of why the world is the way it is, but to describe our existence in the world, our various modes of being-in-the-world, which comes before conscious reflection and theorizing.

CHAPTER 2

PERCEPTION

EMPIRICISM

Phenomenology, as we saw in the last chapter, is an attempt to get away from the theoretical constructions, of science and philosophy, by which we seek to gain intellectual control of our existence, and to return to simple descriptions of our pre-reflective involvement with the world, from which those theoretical constructions themselves derive their meaning. Merleau-Ponty's word for this direct, pre-reflective, involvement is 'perception': so all phenomenology is, in the title of his major work, phenomenology of perception. If phenomenology is an attempt to clarify the meaning of the concepts we use by getting back to the sources of meaning, then perception must be primary, because it is in perception that these sources are to be found. To put it differently, we can only attach meaning to an abstract idea by referring back to our own direct experience of things, that is, to perception. The notion that perception was primary was already to be found in Husserl's later work: for both the later Husserl and Merleau-Ponty, 'perception' was fundamentally a *practical* involvement with things. To perceive something is not just to have an idea of it, but to deal with it in some way.

This is what distinguishes the kind of phenomenology which Merleau-Ponty practised from the empiricism which those who have mainly studied English-speaking philosophy are familiar with. Empiricists too would say that perception was our primary mode of contact with the world – the basis on which all our knowledge of the world rests, and in which the meaning of all our concepts is rooted. But that superficial similarity conceals a deeper difference, and if we can explore that difference in more depth, we can perhaps get a clearer idea of what Merleau-Ponty is seeking to achieve in his philosophy.

First of all, empiricists are concerned above all with the *theory of knowledge*, or epistemology: they want to know what is the most basic kind of evidence which justifies us in claiming to know certain things about the world. Merleau-Ponty, however, is not primarily concerned with our relation to the world as *knowers*, that is, with our *cognitive* relation to things. Cognitive relations to objects are themselves dependent on a more primitive kind of involvement with them, which must be described before we can understand the meaning which more abstract concepts possess. Before we can know what things are in the world, and what characteristics and relations to other things those things have, we must first be involved with things at a much more basic level. Living in the world comes first, knowing about it comes later. For instance, my chair is first of all something to sit on: only because I first have that kind of practical relationship to it can I detach myself to the extent needed to think about it in a more theoretical way, and to seek to know about it – what is it made of, who manufactured it, how likely is it to support my weight, and so on. Questions about knowledge and its evidential support are important, but cannot be separated from other kinds of dealings with the things we seek to know about. To seek to know about a chair presupposes that I know what a chair is, or what is meant by the word 'chair', and the meaning of 'chair' depends on the ways in which I and others interact with the chair practically.

Because empiricists are concerned with cognitive relations in isolation from all the other kinds of ties we have with the world, they take for granted that we know what the world is like: their picture of what the world is like is the picture presupposed by both ordinary common sense and by scientific inquiry. This is what Merleau-Ponty calls the 'objectivist' picture. The world, according to this picture, consists of a huge number of separate objects, all of which occupy space and are spatially related to other objects. In addition to these spatial relations, objects may be *causally* related to other objects: that is, they may affect the position and the properties of these other objects. A billiard ball, for example, strikes another billiard ball with a certain force from a certain direction, and this causes the second billiard ball to move a certain distance in a certain direction. Or a flame applied to a piece of wax causes the wax to melt and change its shape, colour and other properties.

One of the kinds of object in the world, according to objectivism, is that which we call 'human beings': they are members of a biological species. Among the causal relations in the world are the relations between other sorts of objects and human beings, in particular those which cause human beings to *perceive* the other objects. Light is reflected, for instance, from my pen and reaches my eyes, which are open. I am thereby caused to see the pen: the particular wavelength of the light which reaches my eyes causes me to see the pen as having a certain colour (say, blue). Contact between the surface of the pen and the nerve endings in my fingers causes me to feel it as smooth, solid and cylindrical. If I drop the pen on a hard surface, the impact results in sound waves reaching my ears, which causes me to be aware of a particular sort of sound. Other causal relations may cause me to be aware of the smell or the taste of things. The effect of objects on me *via* my sense-organs is what empiricists mean by 'perception'. And the perceiver, or 'perceiving subject', is simply the end of this chain of causes and effects which starts from the object perceived.

Still thinking along the same lines, we can see that our perception of things on this view of it is *indirect*. Seeing, hearing, touching, tasting or smelling the pen involves a chain of processes going on between it and the perceiving subject. Light waves affect my nervous system in a particular way, which in turn causes messages to be sent along the nerves to my brain. Only when they reach the brain am I said to 'see' the pen. So what we call 'my seeing the pen' is really, they conclude, seeing the representation of the pen which eventually reaches me. A comparison might be with the way in which we talk about 'seeing the Cup Final on television', when what we strictly mean is seeing the representation of the Cup Final on the television screen which is caused by the chain of processes going on between the camera and the receiver. Similar things can be said about the other senses. To perceive an object, on this view, really means to have representations, or 'sense-data' or 'ideas', of it, caused by the way it acts upon the perceiver's sense organs.

Not only is perception indirect in this sense, it is also analysable into different components. I am aware of the colour of the pen through my eyes, but of its texture through my sense of touch, of its taste through my taste-buds, and so on. So I have colour sense-data, tactile sense-data, gustatory sense-data, olfactory sense-data, auditory sense-data, all of which have to be combined to make my representation of the pen as such. Even if we restrict ourselves to one sense, the sense of sight, for example, we get different visual sense-data from different angles – how the pen looks from one angle is different from how it looks from another. What we call 'perceiving the pen', on this view, therefore, is not so much perceiving the pen itself and as a whole, as putting together ('associating') a number of distinct representations, caused by different properties of the pen, to make a compound representation of the object as a whole. What we actually see, we might say, is not the pen, but these different representations of it: the idea of the pen as a single object which 'has' a certain colour, shape, texture, smell etc. is in a way a misinterpretation of this 'compound idea' of a collection as if it were a 'simple idea' of a singular object. (This view is very clearly expressed in the writings of one of the greatest of all empiricists, the seventeenth-century English philosopher John Locke, for instance in his *Essay concerning Human Understanding*, Book II, Chapter XXIII, section 1.)

There is nothing wrong with this view of perception, if what we are concerned with is to give a scientific explanation of what goes on when we perceive. Indeed, it is hard to see what else one could say, other than something broadly similar to this, if we want to give a scientific account of perception. We have to explain how we perceive different properties of the object, in terms of its effect on different sense organs in ourselves, and in other cases in terms of the different effects which it has on the same sense-organ from different angles and distances. An explanation of how perception takes place must trace the chain of causes and effects between the object and the perceiver, and in that way must imply that perception is indirect and representational. And perception, interpreted in this way, is essentially *passive*: the perceiving 'subject' is caused to have a representation, that is, must have that representation if they are in the appropriate place and situation (for example, they cannot avoid seeing the pen if they are near enough to it, looking in its direction, are not blind and have their eyes open). This is important, too, from the point of view of the empiricists' epistemological interests, since the passivity of perception is a kind of guarantee that it provides us with true beliefs about the object perceived. To imagine a pen is an active process, in which the mind 'creates' the idea, but to see a real pen is a matter of passively receiving the representation of one which comes into us because of the effects of what really exists on our eyes, without any creative activity on our part. The Latin word *data* (as in 'sense-data') literally means 'what is given': on the empiricist view, we start from what is 'given' to us when our senses are active, and construct a picture of the world from these 'given' elements.

Whatever its virtues as a *scientific* account of what goes on when we perceive something, however, it is hopelessly confused if it is offered as a *philosophical* account of what perception is, which is what the empiricists present it as. For one thing, it is viciously circular. Any scientific theory has to be established by empirical evidence, that is, by evidence based on what we perceive. That presupposes that we already know what counts as 'perception': so science cannot be used, without circularity, to clarify what counts as perception. Given that we understand what is meant by 'perception', we can use empirical evidence to support a particular *explanation* of what goes on when a human being perceives something. But the understanding of what we mean by that term can only be based on philosophical reflection on a description, without assumptions, of our actual perceptual experience. Perception is not *knowledge* about the world, but the mode of access to the world on which knowledge must be based.

Knowledge about the world, about the objects in the world and the relations between them, must come ultimately from the individual experience of human beings. Scientists are themselves human beings, each of whom experiences the world first from his or her own point of view. Science arises when they exchange these individual perspectives on the world with each other in an attempt to arrive at a picture of the world which is *impersonal*, in the sense that it is no individual's property, but represents the world in a way which different individuals can all accept as valid. To take a simple example: a tree may look enormous to a small man, but not very tall to a tall man. Their individual perspectives on the height of the tree are 'subjective' representations affected by their individual relationship to the tree. An 'objective' (or more 'scientific') account of the tree can be arrived at by measuring it, since the results of measurement will be accepted by both as giving a valid statement about the height of the tree. The tree is, say, 4 metres tall, and that statement is equally acceptable to a man who is only 1.5 metres tall and someone who is 2 metres tall.

We arrive at an 'objective' or scientific account of things, then, by as it were transcending our individual perspectives, stepping outside our own individual point of view and looking at the world, including ourselves, in a more impersonal way. But the fact remains that the perceptions we start from are experienced 'from the inside'. We don't experience ourselves as just one more object in the world, but as the point of view from which we perceive other objects. If we are to understand the roots of science, we need to start by describing the world as we experience it in this way, from the inside, before we even begin to be able to construct a scientific framework to explain that world and that experience. It might seem easy to describe this 'world of perception': after all, it is the world we all participate in – even scientists and philosophers participate in it when they are not doing science or philosophy. But in the radio talks which he gave in 1948, Merleau-Ponty tries to show that the perceptual world is in fact largely 'unknown territory as long as we remain in the practical or utilitarian attitude', and that it needs 'much time and effort, as well as culture . . . to lay this world bare' (Merleau-Ponty 2004: 39). The prestige in which we hold science, supported by a philosophical tradition which exalts mathematical reason and intellect over the senses, leads us to think that the real world is the one which science reveals to us. The time and effort he speaks of is that involved in the struggle to free ourselves from this framework and to look at the world afresh. (This struggle, he suggests, characterizes much of modern art as well as phenomenological philosophy.) We have to 'rediscover the world in which we live, yet which we are always prone to forget' (ibid.).

This is not to deny the value of science. As he explains in his radio talks, what Merleau-Ponty is attacking is not science, but 'the dogmatism of a science that thinks itself capable of absolute and complete knowledge' (2004: 45). Science itself, he points out, has changed in the twentieth century, with such developments as Einstein's theory of relativity and quantum theory. What we might call 'classical' modern science, the physics of such innovators as Galileo and Newton, given philosophical support above all by Descartes, saw science as 'penetrating to the heart of things, to the object as it is in itself . . . to an object free of all human traces, just as God would see it' (Merleau-Ponty 2004: 44–5). But since the end of the nineteenth century, Merleau-Ponty argues, scientists themselves have increasingly seen that idea of absolute objectivity as unattainable. Human beings always start from a particular situation, from where they are as individuals and as members of a community which is itself situated in a particular culture and historical period. That is why we have to try, difficult though it is, to get beneath the abstractions of science to the subjective experiences from which it emerges.

When we make that effort, we discover, above all, that the world we perceive, unlike the world of scientific theory, is not a collection of separate objects, but a whole, in which the way we perceive one object is always affected by its relation to others – it points beyond itself, and thus has a *meaning*. In short, it is a *world*. In the objectivist picture, each object can be conceived of as distinct from every other, and so as having *determinate* properties – as being definitely, for instance, one colour rather than another. Furthermore, the individual objects too are perceived as wholes, not as collections of 'ideas' or 'sense-data'. That is, the qualities which an individual object has are experienced not separately and distinctly, but as affecting each other. We can see this as soon as we begin to reflect, without making any objectivist assumptions, on what our perceptual experience is actually like. Merleau-Ponty, as a phenomenologist, has to depend, not on logical argument, but on a simple appeal to what his readers will (he thinks) see as soon as they do remove the veil of assumptions about what perception *must* be like, and attend to what they do experience.

Consider some examples which Merleau-Ponty gives in the early chapters of *Phenomenology of Perception*. The particular red colour which he perceives in his carpet, he argues, is what it is in virtue of the play of light on it, and of the fact that it is a 'woolly' red (as opposed to, say, the red of a piece of cotton or silk or metal). Or he takes the famous Müller-Lyer illusion, discussed in the psychology of perception. Two lines are measurably of the same length, and if seen separately and in a different context would be experienced as of equal length. But if they are presented in parallel to each other, and with arrowheads attached to each, pointing in the opposite direction in one line from in the other, then they are experienced as being of different lengths. (For a visual representation of the illusion, see Merleau-Ponty 2002: 6.) Or again, if one is walking along the sea shore and sees a ship in the distance, the funnel or masts may seem to be part of the forest adjacent to the shore; but there comes a point when they are suddenly seen as part of the ship. In all these cases, we experience the world, and the things in it, as wholes, in which each part has a meaning derived from its relation to the whole.

These examples are of the kind given by the Gestalt psychologists who, as explained in Chapter 1, had a great influence on Merleau-Ponty before he discovered the later Husserl. The Gestaltists argued, as was said earlier, that perception was not of a collection of separate sense-data, but of things and situations as wholes, in which each part was affected by its place in the whole. In this, Merleau-Ponty thought, the Gestaltists were right. Where they went wrong was in thinking of this as an empirical discovery about human psychology, whereas in fact it was a philosophical claim about the nature of human perception. Gestalt theory was, in his opinion, a hybrid between psychology and philosophy. What was needed was to recognize that these points about the holistic character of perception emerged, not from empirical research, but from attempting to describe without presuppositions what it is like to perceive. Gestalt psychology, Merleau-Ponty argues, fails to see that the 'psychological atomism' which it criticizes is only one example of a view based on objectivist prejudices, and that acceptance of its account of perception is not merely the substitution of one psychological theory for another, but a rejection of the whole objectivist framework for thinking of human experience (Merleau-Ponty 2002: 59).

Rejecting that framework means, as said before, accepting that science itself must be 'situated', that we perceive always from some perspective. Our account of the world is given *from our own point of view*. Some things are nearer to us than others, some are experienced as above others, or to the left or right of others, and all these features of the world as experienced depend on the relation between our position and that of what we see. It is because we always perceive things as they appear from a certain angle and distance that 'phenomena', objects as we directly experience them before we begin to think about them, appear as indeterminate and ambiguous. In the world of scientific theory, by contrast, things always have definite qualities, in particular definite *quantitative* or measurable properties.

The empiricist notion of perception as representational, of the immediate objects of perception as 'sense-data', 'ideas' or, to use the word which Merleau-Ponty himself uses, 'sensations' was, he maintains, philosophically untenable. The 'sensations' which were supposed to function as the units or building blocks of experience were thought to be both objects of perception and states of the perceiver – they had to be thought of in this way if they were to fulfil their alleged function. They must be states of the perceiver, because of the part which they play in the causal chain leading from the object to our perception of it. The object affects our sense organs, thus causing the 'sensation', which is necessary if we are to perceive. But they must also be what we immediately perceive, since perception on this view is supposed to be an indirect process – we see the pen *via* our inner representation of it (the sensation), so in that sense what we *directly* perceive must be the sensation, rather than the pen as it is in itself. It is easy to see, however, that there is a contradiction in this theory: sensations *cannot* be at the same time both states of the perceiver and what he or she perceives. What we perceive must be external to us as perceivers: that is what distinguishes perceiving from imagining or hallucinating.

Those who hold a sense-datum theory would at this point object that part of their point is precisely that we can't distinguish, within our subjective experiences, those which are perceptions from those which are imaginings or hallucinations. What is 'given' to us in our experience, they would say, might be something which really exists, or it might be something imaginary or illusory, and there are no qualitative differences between these experiences. From a phenomenological point of view, however, Merleau-Ponty would reply that this is simply not so. If we reflect on our actual experience, without presuppositions derived from any philosophical or scientific theory, then we can clearly distinguish the experience of actual perception from that of imagination. When we perceive, what we experience is never an atomistic 'sensation', but part of a world, as we have seen already, and its character is affected by its relations to other parts of the world. The world is experienced, to use Merleau-Ponty's own word, as 'inexhaustible' – as stretching beyond my immediate visual field, and as always offering more to be experienced. When we imagine or hallucinate, however, there is in the object imagined only what is immediately presented, what is 'put into it' by ourselves as imaginers. Indeed, he might say that imagining and hallucinating make sense only by contrast with perceiving: our basic mode of experience is perception of the actual world, and we use the concepts of imagination or hallucination only when our experience falls short of that standard.

If this is so, then perception is not indirect at all: it opens out directly on to the real, inexhaustible world. Sensations may play some role in the scientific explanation of the possibility of perception, but they are not what we perceive. What I see is my pen, or the red carpet on my floor, or the lines of the Müller-Lyer illusion. I see, or otherwise perceive, such things as parts of a unified world, which gain meaning for me from the role which they play in that world, in much the same way that the elements of a painting may get meaning from their contribution to the whole. And each object is itself seen as a unified whole: I don't have to put together different representations of my pen to form the 'complex idea' of it as a single thing, for example, but directly experience it as such.

'INTELLECTUALISM'

Empiricists do make an effort to explain the unity and coherence of the world that we perceive. They talk, for instance, as we have seen already, of 'association' of one idea with another. An example might be this: having the 'simple ideas' (sensations) of black colour, cylindrical shape, smooth surface, silver tip, I might 'associate' or combine these ideas to form the 'compound idea' of a single object called a 'pen'. But this, Merleau-Ponty argues, will not do. These 'simple ideas' would be combined for no reason: the connections which the mind made between them would be entirely arbitrary, by the empiricists' own theory. According to empiricism, we start with simple ideas or sensations, which simply come into our mind: the mind in this is entirely passive. There can be no intrinsic connection therefore between any two ideas. The only way in which there could be an intrinsic connection which would *justify* us in associating them would be if we started with the idea of a unified thing, and saw its colour, shape, texture and so on as different properties of this unified thing. The association of different ideas cannot constitute the 'meaning' of something as a unified object, since that meaning is already presupposed in our ability to associate (cf. Merleau-Ponty 2002: 18).

Another attempt by empiricists to allow for the unity and meaningfulness of the world we perceive is to say that *memory* plays a role in perception. In seeing my desk as a unified thing, with the things on it having a meaning in relation to each other, I am, these empiricists would say, influenced by my memories of the same desk in the past. Past experience helps to organize present perception. But this, Merleau-Ponty argues, faces the same kind of objection as the theory of the association of ideas. There is a circularity about it. In order for memories to have any influence on present experience, the perceiver must experience the present as organized in the same way as past experience was. The present experience has to be compared with the past, and so has to have an organization like the one previously experienced. In other words, memory presupposes the organization of experience, and so cannot explain why experience is organized. Both the theory of association and that of the role of memory reveal what is basically wrong with empiricism. Empiricism makes our experience of the world a succession of unrelated perceptions, and so has no room for a *subject* of experience who could relate them to each other to form a unified world.

Other philosophers in the modern western tradition have also seen the weaknesses in the kind of empiricism described above, though in Merleau-Ponty's opinion they have not gone far enough in their criticism, since they have taken over too many of the empiricists' false assumptions. The philosophers he has in mind are those he usually calls 'intellectualists'. He does not mention particular names, but it is fair to presume that one outstanding example of an 'intellectualist' philosopher would be Kant. Kant was impressed by David Hume's empiricist critique of the rationalist philosophers who thought we could arrive at substantive conclusions about the structure of reality ('metaphysics') by pure a priori reasoning in the mathematical style. Hume, he said, 'woke him from his dogmatic slumbers'. But Hume's radical empiricism seemed to Kant to have problems of its own. Like other empiricists, Hume took our experience to consist of a succession of sensations ('impressions', as he called them), which formed the basis on which our more abstract ideas were constructed. Any alleged idea which could not be related to impressions was empty of meaning.

But this created problems for some crucial ideas, like that of causality, a unified space and time, or a unified self. To say that A causes B, for instance, seems to be to say that there is some special kind of connection between A and B, that the sequence 'A–B' is a unified whole: but, on Hume's account of experience, we perceive A and B separately, and the only connection between them is that our perception of A comes before that of B. So is the idea of causal connection an empty or meaningless idea? That is an odd thing to say, given that the idea of causality is such an important part, not only of science but even of our common-sense view of the world. All that Hume could say was that the idea of causality should not be considered as based on *reason*, as a rational intuition into real connections in the world, but as arising from our own *habits of thinking*. If we see events of type A regularly followed by events of type B, we get into the habit of expecting B when we experience A, and that is what gives meaning to the idea that A 'causes' B. (Hume gives similar accounts of other ideas, such as that of a unified self.)

This account means that the idea of causality is not a *rational* conception which has an *objective* reference to the real world, but something based purely on our own *subjective* habits: in a sense, it is a kind of fiction. Kant could not accept this, given the central role which the idea plays in distinguishing between subjective sequences in our experiences and objective relationships in the world. So he proposed that we think of such conceptions as causality as part of the necessary structure which we impose on the world as we experience it in order to make that distinction, without which we should not have a notion of 'experience' at all. Such conceptions, and the principles derived from them (like the causal principle: that every event has a cause), are not merely irrational habits, but are part of the necessary structure of our thought: the framework in terms of which we interpret the flow of our experience in order to make it a coherent picture of a world. Knowledge of the world must, as the empiricists held, start from what is given, but what is given must be structured and interpreted before it can be the basis of anything worthy of the name 'knowledge'.

Merleau-Ponty has some sympathy with this sort of intellectualism, which at least recognizes, unlike the empiricists, that our experience is not of a collection of objects, but of a unified world, and that this feature of our experience must be accounted for in some way. The trouble with intellectualism is that it shares too much with the very empiricism which it claims to oppose. It does not start from a phenomenological description of what our experience is actually like, but from a conception of experience which is based on certain presuppositions derived from the scientific theories by which we explain experience. Above all, it assumes, like the empiricists, that experience consists of a flow of impressions or sensations, the result of the impact of the outside world on our senses. This is the unstructured 'matter' of our experience. Then the problem becomes to explain how this 'matter' is given the 'form' which it must have if it is to constitute an experience of a world. The only solution, if one accepts this starting-point, seems to be to say that *we*, or our minds, supply the form. A comparison might be with what happens when we are given a puzzle-picture like the 'duck-rabbit', and then see it *as* either a duck or a rabbit. The form of the world, on this view, is not actually *in* the world at all, but in the ways we think about it. The difference between Kant and Hume (and it is an important difference) is that for the former these ways of thinking are necessary structures of any experience, whereas for the latter they are simply habits by which we happen to organize our perceptions.

PHENOMENOLOGY AND THE UNITY OF THE EXPERIENCED WORLD

Neither Kant's nor Hume's views satisfy Merleau-Ponty, since neither is based on phenomenological description. Both start from the wrong end, as if it could be taken for granted that there is an objective world as described in science, that we were one of the objects in that world, and that our experience is the result of the causal effects of other objects on objects of our type. But that 'objectivist' view derives whatever meaning it has *from* our experience: as has been said before, scientists are human beings, who start from their own subjective experience of things and develop an objective view by comparing their subjective experiences with each other. Experience itself is prior to any scientific theories which try to explain it. To put it differently, how we think about the world is rooted in how we interact with it before we think, and so our intellectual thoughts cannot be used to explain away that pre-reflective experience. In an address to the French Philosophical Society in 1946 on 'The Primacy of Perception and Its Philosophical Consequences', Merleau-Ponty asserts 'that our relation to the world is not that of a thinker to an object of thought', and that we cannot conceive 'the perceiving subject as a consciousness which "interprets", "deciphers", or "orders" a sensible matter according to an ideal law which it possesses' (1964a: 12).

When we think about the world, we take a detached view of it: we as it were step back from it to consider what the relevant facts of the situation are, so that we can then construct a theory or a statement about those facts. If that theory or statement is to be adequate, we need to be as objective or disinterested as we can be about the facts. If I am a detective, for instance, trying to work out who murdered Sir Archibald, I need first of all to review the possible suspects. Who had the motive and the opportunity? That involves analysing the situation into its component parts. If I am to solve the crime, I must set aside any personal feelings, of like or dislike, for example, which I may have about any of these suspects, and consider in a detached fashion how the components of the situation which I have analysed can most plausibly be put together to form a satisfactory theory. In the old cliché, I must put together the separate pieces of the jigsaw to make a whole and coherent picture.

This is what is involved in thinking about experience. But the experience we think about is not like that. When I first encounter the crime scene, I experience it as a whole, and the various elements in it as having a meaning for me in relation to that whole. Sir Archibald's body is slumped over his desk in the study, obviously stabbed in the back. He is obviously dead, indeed murdered, or at least killed by someone else. These meanings which I find in the elements of the situation (described by the concepts of 'death' and 'murder', or that of 'being slumped over' the desk, rather than of, say, 'leaning over it') are there in the situation itself – I *find* them in it, rather than *impose* them on it. It is not an arbitrary matter, like seeing the duck-rabbit either as a duck or as a rabbit; I don't have any choice about how I see it. Of course, these meanings which I find in the situation have to do with human concepts. In some cases (though probably not in this one) they may be relative to some particular human culture: someone coming from a culture in which computers did not exist, and in which there was no conception of how they might be used, would not find the same meaning in the object on which I am writing these words as I do. But this means, not that I 'impose' the meaning 'computer' on this object in front of me, but that the nature of my interaction with it, in the context of our culture, means that I inescapably interpret it in this way.

In the passage cited a little earlier, Merleau-Ponty goes on to say, 'Matter is "pregnant" with its form, which is to say that in the final analysis every perception takes place within a certain horizon and ultimately in the "world" ' (1964a: 12). The intellectualists, unlike the empiricists, do at least allow for the role played by the subject of experience, and so can see the world and the objects in it as having meaning *for* the subject. The trouble is that their 'subject' is conceived of as standing outside the world of experience, and *imposing* the meaning on that world. It is a 'transcendental', not a 'situated' subject. But the very nature of perception implies that a perceiving, as opposed to a thinking, subject must be situated somewhere *in* the world of space and time: to perceive is always, as said earlier, to perceive from a particular perspective or point of view. And this is why the world is inevitably perceived as a structured and meaningful whole: it is because it is not simply an object of abstract thought for us, but the place in which we live. We move about the world, make use of the objects in it, respond to situations emotionally, act in order to change it, and so on. All these and other ways of interacting with the world give rise to its meaningfulness, so that the meanings of things, in a sense, exist neither 'inside' our minds nor in the world itself, but in the space between us and the world. If we did not exist in the way we do, the world and the objects in it would have no meaning; but since we do exist in the way we do, and are actively engaged in the world, the world and things are necessarily perceived as meaningful. And it is only because we experience the world as a unified and meaningful whole that we can then construct scientific and other thoughts about the world, seen as if from nowhere. The idea of an objective world has meaning for us only because we first experience the world subjectively. What is wrong with both empiricism and intellectualism is that they *take for granted* the scientific view of the world, without seeing that view as the result of pre-scientific experience. This has important consequences, as we shall see in later chapters, for our philosophical account of many aspects of our experience, but especially of human nature and human behaviour.

Perception, therefore, as Merleau-Ponty uses that term, is not a matter of passively receiving the 'representations' given from outside, and then interpreting them. It is a *direct* contact with the world, and that contact takes the form of active engagement with the things around us. Things have the meaning for us that they do because of our interest in them, which shapes the character of our engagement with them. Sometimes (as when, for instance, we are engaged in science) that interest may be purely cognitive: we want to know the truth about them, and to understand why they are the way they are, independently of any value which they may have for us. My pen, considered in this way, is seen solely as a black plastic object with a metallic tip. I may be interested in the constitution of the plastic of which it is made, which is the same as that of other plastic objects: through this knowledge, I may be able to understand how the plastic can be shaped into this kind of object, and differently shaped when it is made into, say, an ashtray. This kind of interest is concerned with the pen simply as a member of a certain class of objects, made of the same material: the pen itself, as an individual thing, is not of interest from this kind of 'scientific' point of view.

But our engagement with the world is, of course, not purely cognitive, intellectual or theoretical. In large part, our interest in the world is emotional, practical, aesthetic, imaginative, economic and so on. The pen may mean something to me, perhaps, because it was given to me by my wife: I see it, not just as 'a pen made of black plastic', but as 'Hellen's present'. As such, it has an *individual* meaning: it is not just any old pen, but a specific pen which I value emotionally because of my emotional relationship with the donor. The pen also has a *practical* meaning for me: it is a tool which I can use for certain purposes, a writing instrument. This meaning is not purely individual: it is an essential part of our shared concept of a 'pen' that a pen is something which is used in this way – pens can be of different sizes, shapes and colours, but what they all have in common is this use.

The pen may also have an aesthetic meaning, as an attractively (or unattractively) designed object; or an imaginative meaning – I might, in a flight of fancy, see it as a submarine, or it might suggest ways of designing some new kind of machine. Or it might have an economic meaning: it is something which cost a certain amount of money to buy, and which could, if necessary be sold for a certain price. The same object can have all these different kinds of meaning, and more: and can carry different meanings at the same time – this is the pen which I use to write letters with, and which I am fond of because it was the first present I was given by my wife. Some of these meanings will be purely personal to me: it is likely that the emotional, aesthetic and imaginative meanings are, for example. Others will usually be shared with others: this will usually be true of the cognitive, practical and economic meanings. Everyone who speaks the same language as me will know what is meant by a 'black plastic cylinder', or by a 'pen', in the sense of a writing instrument, or by an 'expensive' or a 'cheap' pen. These shared meanings are of the kind which are expressed in a language, which is itself, as Wittgenstein's argument against the possibility of a private language shows, essentially shared. But things can have meanings for us which are not necessarily expressed in words: even at the most basic, pre-reflective, and so pre-linguistic, level, our experience is always of a meaningful world.

Perception in one sense creates the world perceived, but in another sense does not. The world I perceive is, in one sense, *my* world, and so different from *your* world. It is a *meaningful* world, and the meanings it has are the meanings which *I* find in it. Unless it had these meanings, it would not be a *world* at all, just a collection of unrelated objects: the meaning of one object in the world is dependent on its relation to other objects and their meanings. To call something a 'desk' is not to refer to the materials it is made of, or its shape or design, but to its function: a desk is something which supports other things, usually things used in a particular kind of work – things like computers, papers, pens, staplers, books and the like. My computer, in turn, is the kind which sits on desks – it is a 'desktop' computer.

The papers, books and so on arranged on the desk are those which are relevant to what I am currently writing on the computer. The wall behind the desk is one of the walls of my study, where I do this kind of work. One could continue, but the point is now clear. My world at the moment is unified by the varying contributions of all the elements in it to the task in which I am currently engaged: their interrelated meanings give coherence to my world.

My activities thus, in that sense, constitute my present world: it has the meanings it has by virtue of what I am doing. But I can only do what I am now doing because the world, and the things in it, have a character independent of my wishes and interests. I can put my computer on the desk only because the desk is strong enough and designed in such a way as to support it: whether it has these characteristics or not is not in any sense the result of my choice, but of facts about the world. Similarly with other elements in the situation. In that sense, the world is not purely my world, and the meanings of objects in it are meanings which I *find*, rather than meanings which I *create*.

We return to the point already made. Perceiving is neither, as it is for the objectivist, passively receiving representations from objects; nor, as it is for philosophical idealists, creating the world from the ideas in my mind. The perceiver is *in* the world, but not in the same way that pure objects are: the perceiver is a subject who acts on the world as well as being acted upon by it. This, as we shall see in the next chapter, has important consequences for our view of our own position in the world. It means that we are essentially *embodied subjects*.

CHAPTER 3

EMBODIMENT

THE ROOTS OF OBJECTIVISM

Science is the pursuit of knowledge – the very word 'science' comes from the mediaeval Latin *scientia*, which means 'knowledge'. When we have knowledge about anything, we are not simply expressing our own personal opinion about it, or how it appears to us from our point of view, but *how it is in itself*. When I say that a jumbo jet in the sky looks tiny, I am simply expressing how it looks to me on the ground, at a great distance from it. But to someone standing near the plane, on the airport runway before it takes off, the same jumbo jet looks huge. Both of these apparently conflicting judgements are correct, so that they are not really in conflict, as long as we are both talking about how the plane looks to us, from our particular perspective. But if we want to describe what the actual size of the jumbo jet is (and in that sense to be 'scientific' about it), these particular perspectives are not good enough – they are too 'subjective'. The jumbo in itself is x metres long from nose to tail, has a wing span of y metres, and stands z metres above the runway. Describing it in that way is not saying how its size appears to one or other observer, from where they happen to be, but describing something which is independent of any observer – which is 'objective'.

If science aims at knowledge, it must seek to describe the world in that objective way: to use the phrase of Thomas Nagel's which has been mentioned already, it must aim at the 'view from nowhere'. As Merleau-Ponty puts it, in a phrase which has also been quoted in an earlier chapter, it must aim 'to gain access to an object free of all human traces, just as God would see it' (2004: 45). The 'view from nowhere' has sometimes been described as the 'God's eye view', since

God, as conceived of in traditional Christian theology, is supposed to 'transcend' the world, to look at the world, as it were, from a position outside of it, and so to comprehend it in a way which is not limited by any particular perspective.

The revolutionary thinkers of the sixteenth and seventeenth centuries who in effect founded the modern scientific view of the world did so by recognizing, perhaps unconsciously, this need to adopt a view from nowhere if we were to have genuine knowledge about the world and ourselves. This recognition was given its clearest philosophical formulation in the writings of Descartes (1595–1650). Descartes was dissatisfied with what he was taught at the distinguished Jesuit school he attended, even though it represented the most respectable account of things available at the time. His dissatisfaction came from his sense that all this weight of learning represented in the end only someone's opinion, supported only by tradition and authority and a naïve reliance on what our senses appeared to tell us. The sun, for instance, was supposed to go round the earth, which remained motionless at the centre of the cosmos. The basis for this belief was partly that that is what respected authorities, including the ancient Greek astronomers and some passages in the Bible, had said, and partly because it seems obvious that this is how things are – we seem to *see* the sun moving, rising in the east in the morning and setting in the west in the evening. But how can we be sure that these provide us with good grounds for our belief? Might not the ancient authorities be just mistaken? And do not we find very often that what our senses appear to tell us is just deceptive?

What was needed, Descartes thought, was to start afresh, and to find a criterion which would enable us to decide without doubt which beliefs we held were true representations of how things were, and which were not. His method for arriving at that criterion was to go through all the kinds of things he already believed – beliefs based on his senses, beliefs based on mathematical reasoning, even the very basic assumptions which seem necessary for sanity, such as the assumption that there is a physical world at all, including one's own body. In each case, he would see if there were possible (not just reasonable, but barely possible) grounds for doubting them, and if there were, then he would set them aside as if they were false. In this way, he hoped he could reach at least one belief which it was absolutely impossible to doubt, however hard he tried: the criterion for believing it would then give him a criterion which could be relied on in other cases too. The whole structure of beliefs could be rebuilt on this sounder foundation, and so would constitute genuine *knowledge*, rather than just received opinion. The one belief he found which met this standard, as most people who have studied even a little of the history of philosophy know, was the belief in his own existence as a purely thinking being: 'I think, therefore I am.' This could not be doubted, because even to doubt it was to affirm its truth: to doubt that one is a thinking being is possible only if one *is* a thinking being, since doubting is a form of thinking. And equally obviously to doubt whether one exists is possible only if one *does* exist.

It is worth looking more closely at what is going on in Descartes's method of doubt, both for its own sake and because it helps us to understand Merleau-Ponty's position better. In doubting his various beliefs about the world, Descartes is, as it might be put, stepping back mentally from his ordinary involvement with things around him. I believe that I am sitting at my desk, working on my computer; my belief is based on what my senses tell me, and so implies a certain kind of involvement with the desk, the computer and other elements in my surrounding environment. I normally rely on my senses because they respond to the things I see, hear, touch, taste and smell. In doubting the reliability of my senses as Descartes does, not just on occasion but as a general principle, I am mentally suspending this bond between me and objects. This is most obvious when I get to what Descartes calls 'hyperbolical' (or extreme) doubt – when I suspend my very basic belief in the existence of a world outside myself, and even in the existence of my own body as part of that world. In accepting only his own existence as a thinking thing, as free from all doubt, Descartes is, as it were, retreating into his own thoughts, and regarding his existence as a thinker, a 'subject', as totally separate from any involvement with the physical world. This is why Descartes moves from his conclusion, that only 'I think, therefore I am' is beyond doubt, to an argument for his 'dualism', his belief that his essential self is to be identified only with his mind and is distinct from any physical or bodily existence he may have.

Given that, his own body becomes, not part of himself, but an object in the physical world like any other, and like any other object something which is external to him as a thinking subject. It is something 'out there', to be observed, just like his chair or his desk, not something he has any internal connection with. So the ultimate conclusion of Descartes's thinking is the picture of himself as something entirely disembodied, outside the world, looking at the things in the world in an entirely detached way. In that sense, he, as a thinking subject, has no situation within the world, because it is our bodies that give us a situation: my present perspective on the world is determined by where my body now is, sitting at my desk in the study (rather than, say, standing in the street outside looking in through the window). That perspective decides how things look to me – the apparent shape of the desk, for example, depends on the angle I am observing it from. In this way, Descartes's thinking subject has the kind of 'God's eye view', or 'view from nowhere' that was spoken of earlier, and that is why Descartes can be said to have given a clear presentation, probably the clearest possible presentation, of the classical scientific view of the world.

The detachment of the thinker from the world that is thought about is a detachment from all forms of involvement with that world. If I am a pure observer, standing outside the world which is observed, I do not have any ties of interest, emotion, meaning or value with the things in that world. From a Cartesian point of view, my computer is just an object with certain observable properties. It is not something I find practically useful, and so attach a value or a meaning to: these are properties which it could have only in relation to me, as a fellow-participant in the world. Even some of its apparent observable properties are not really part of the object itself, since they depend on its relation to me and to my position (or the position of my body) within the world. These are what John Locke called an object's 'secondary qualities', like colour, taste and smell: what colour an object has, for instance, depends on the lighting conditions in which one observes it, rather than on anything intrinsic to the object. To see it as coloured at all is possible only for a being equipped with certain kinds of sense-organs: human beings for the most part have the rods and cones in their eyes which make colour vision possible, whereas cows (I understand) do not, and so do not see objects as distinguished by colour. The world as it is in itself, the world as seen by God from outside, has only those properties which do not depend on any relation to a particular being observing from a particular perspective. This means in effect that it has only what Locke calls 'primary qualities' – the qualities which can be measured, like size and shape, since we can all, no matter what our individual perspective, agree on what is measurable.

So the classical scientific view of the world, what Merleau-Ponty calls the 'objectivist' view, is of things as 'value-free', as having no 'meaning', and as having only those properties which are quantitative or measurable in some way. Concepts of value, meaning and qualitative properties are purely 'subjective' – attributed to things not because they are 'in the things themselves', but because of the relation in which they stand to us as beings within the world. And the scientific understanding of the world must be only in terms of the quantitative relations between things. Why do the earth and other planets go round the sun in elliptical orbits? Because of the gravitational attraction of the sun, which can be measured, according to Newton, in terms of the distance of the sun from the planet and the relative masses of the two objects. From a scientific point of view, there is no *purpose* in planetary motion, and it is neither a *good* nor a *bad* thing, since notions like 'purpose' or 'good' or 'bad' depend for their meaning only on human, subjective, responses to things. (We shall come back to this point about scientific understanding, particularly of human behaviour, in Chapter 4.)

Most crucially, from our present point of view, this objectivist picture implies that the observer's own body is just one other object in the world to be observed. This is not normally how, in our non-scientific or pre-scientific way, we regard our own bodies. The fingers that I am typing these words with are *my* fingers: I feel the pressure when I touch the computer keyboard with them, in a way I don't when you touch the keyboard. Furthermore, these fingers are not just something I observe, but something I *use*, in order to type what I want to type. In general, for each of us, 'my body' is not something to be merely observed, but something which we 'live', something which is part of ourselves, and essential to our engagement with the world.

THE LIMITS OF OBJECTIVISM

The idea of an objective, value-free, meaning-free world, and of a distinction between how the world looks to each of us from our own individual position and how the world actually is in itself, seems, for the reasons given earlier, to be essential to any conception of the pursuit of knowledge, that is, of science. And science in this sense is certainly one of the great achievements of humanity: Descartes was surely right to be dissatisfied with views of the world which were merely matters of opinion, with no possibility of deciding objectively which were right and which were wrong opinions. Nevertheless, Merleau-Ponty wants to argue that a purely objectivist account of the world is also ultimately unsatisfactory and misleading in important ways: this is what he calls, in words which we have already quoted, 'the dogmatism of a science that thinks itself capable of absolute and complete knowledge' (2004: 45). The scientific point of view is right in its proper context, but it becomes misleading when it is taken out of that proper context.

Why does Merleau-Ponty say that? We can begin to see if we go back to Descartes. Descartes, in proposing the method of doubt, imagined that it was possible to progressively withdraw (mentally, at least) from all our usual connections with the world, and to end up in the only really secure position, the one in which we had no connection with the world at all and had retreated completely into ourselves. But is that really possible? To doubt is, after all, itself to have a certain kind of involvement with the world: genuine doubt depends on having certain *reasons* for doubting, reasons which I can offer to others to show that my doubt is grounded in something real about my situation. Suppose, for example, I am Macbeth, doubting whether this is a dagger that I see before me. Why do I doubt this? Because there is something 'fishy' about my present apparent perception of a dagger: there is no normal reason for there being a dagger here, for instance. In other words, even the possibility of doubting this particular would-be perception depends on my not doubting other things, such as the conditions under which a dagger would normally be found some-where. To doubt one thing involves *not* doubting others, as Merleau-Ponty argues (cf. Merleau-Ponty 2002: 445). So it is just not possible to doubt the existence of the world as a whole: to be capable of doubt, we must be situated *within* a world, some beliefs about which we do not doubt. We therefore cannot extract ourselves entirely from the world and view it 'from nowhere'.

The development of science itself in the twentieth century, as Merleau-Ponty points out, implies the same conclusion. Quantum mechanics in particular, at least according to some interpretations, requires us to take account of the fact that the scientist's observation of things involves an interaction with them, and so is not completely detached. We can interact with things in the world only if we are our-selves part of the same world. And even without these reminders from quantum theory, we could have worked this out on purely philosoph-ical grounds. Science, after all, depends on experience: it is an attempt to make some kind of rational sense of the world as we experience it. But experience is always *someone's*: each of us, including scientists, must experience the world from his or her own point of view. The very notion of science as 'empirical' thus implies that scientists are situated within the world, not standing outside it in a detached or God-like position. The idea of a 'view from nowhere', when one reflects upon it, is self-contradictory: a 'view' must by definition be from *somewhere*. God, if he exists, cannot *experience* the world as we do, by perception, but must have some kind of all-encompassing intellectual awareness of the world. As far as we are concerned, however, that kind of all-encompassing intellectual awareness is only a kind of abstraction or ideal. In doing science, we do seek to transcend our individual perspectives in order to arrive at a view of things which we can share with other individuals. But the view we end up with is not 'from nowhere', but as Merleau-Ponty sometimes puts it, 'from everywhere' (2002: 79). It is not an *im*personal view so much as an *inter*personal conception – something all competent observers can agree upon.

The objectivist view has certain implications for our conception of ourselves. For Descartes himself, as we have seen already, his arguments implied dualism: the conception of the self as something entirely separate from the physical world which it observes, something purely 'inner' into which we can withdraw when we sever all our connections with the 'external' or material world, a pure 'subject'. One of the fundamental problems with this kind of dualism, however, is how we can account for any interaction between the self and the world. How can we speak of the subject observing the world if it is not part of the world? Relations between things within the physical world can be explained by the laws of physics, but they apply only within the physical world, and so cannot explain the relation between subjects and physical objects. Relations of thoughts within the subject are no doubt governed by their own laws – the laws of logic, or perhaps of psychology. But again these laws cannot explain the relation between the physical and mental worlds. What we call 'observation' seems to become, if Descartes is right, just an intellectual awareness of the *thoughts* or *ideas* of things, and it is only, as Descartes sees it, the goodness of God which allows us to be confident that some of these ideas refer to really existing objects in the material world. So dualism is ultimately incoherent: it was arrived at as part of a project to justify genuine or 'scientific' knowledge of the world, but ends up treating such knowledge either as unattainable or as achievable only thanks to the grace of a God whose own existence may be open to doubt.

These sorts of difficulties have led other objectivist thinkers in a very different direction. Human beings, they would argue, are simply to be identified with one kind of material object, namely a human body, which is itself, like all other material objects, simply a physico-chemical system whose workings can be explained by the laws of physics. This 'materialist' view certainly places human beings within the world, and so gets round the problems we have seen with Descartes's dualism. 'Observation' of things just becomes the impact of things on human sense-organs, which is nothing more than a phys-ical process, explainable by the ordinary laws of physics. Although this avoids some of the most important difficulties in dualism, it runs into equally serious problems of its own. For observation of some-thing surely means something other than passive response to that thing, caused by its impact on our sense-organs. Light-rays can be reflected from something to our eyes, but still we do not *see* that thing: we may for instance be absorbed in our thoughts about other things, or our normal sight may be disturbed by the effect of drugs or alcohol, so that what we see is just a 'buzzing, blooming confusion', rather than a particular object. Observing something is being con-scious of it, and consciousness is, to use a word introduced earlier, 'intentional': we are conscious *of* that thing, and of that thing *under a certain description*. What I am seeing now, for instance, is a computer screen: in order for me to see it, it must of course affect my retina in various ways, but that is not enough for me to be conscious of it *as a computer screen*. For that, I must have the concept of such a screen, and must apply it to what I am seeing now. Perception thus involves some activity on my part, as well as the necessary element of passiv-ity. This is what is meant by saying that there must be a perceiving *subject*, someone who perceives; to put it differently, it is *people* who perceive, not objects which are no more than objects. When the film in a camera, for instance, is affected by the light reaching it through the camera lens, we do not say that the camera, or the film, is 'per-ceiving' anything.

Materialists would say that we can account for the element of sub-jectivity while still regarding the perceivers as objects in the world. When we say, for example, that perceiving involves the having and applying of concepts, we can account for this in terms of brain mech-anisms which obey the laws of physics. If I have the concept of a com-puter screen, it is because I have learned to use these words in a certain way to refer to one of the elements in my experience. This learning involves the operation of certain mechanisms in my brain – the firing of certain neurons in response to certain stimuli and not others. The ways in which these neurological processes involved in learning the meaning of words occur can, the materialists would say, be explained entirely by seeing them as sequences of electro-chemical connections which are governed by the ordinary laws of physics and chemistry – the same laws which apply to the behaviour of other processes in other kinds of object. There is no need, therefore, they would conclude, to postulate anything called a 'subject' of perception, if that means anything more than an object with the special kinds of structures possessed by the human brain.

With much of this, Merleau-Ponty would agree. It is not necessary, he would argue, to think of the 'subject' of perception as having some special and independent kind of existence, in the way Descartes does. (In that sense, he too holds a form of 'materialism' – he does not believe in the existence of anything non-material.) What does the perceiving is indeed a human being, a member of a particular biological species, which is able to perceive only because certain processes go on in his or her brain and nervous system. Nevertheless, the relation between the subject and object of perception, he would say, is not and cannot be the kind of purely causal relation, governed only by the laws of physics and chemistry, which exists between two things which are simply objects in the world. When I, a human being, see the object in front of me now, I see it *as* a computer screen, as something which has a certain *meaning* for me connected with the uses to which I put it, or can put it, in my life. 'Meaning' is not a term belonging to the language of physics: it is not a physical object or quantity, like the wavelength of the light reflected from the screen, which causes me to respond in a particular way. Furthermore, I can attribute the same meaning to objects which do not actually exist, like the fictional computer screen in a story, and, as said before, what does not exist cannot stand in a causal relationship to anything. I distinguish computer screens from other objects which might have many, or even most, of the same properties – the same shape, colour, texture and so on. And I use the same term to refer to objects which differ from each other in respect of one or more of these properties – which have a different shape and/or colour and/or texture from my computer screen. Learning the concept of a computer screen is learning to make such distinctions, and I can do that only as part of learning how to use a computer.

This learning certainly requires certain processes to go on in my brain: if I didn't have a brain, and one of the kind of complexity that human brains usually have, I obviously could not learn to use a computer at all. But it does not follow that that is *all* that is involved in learning a concept like this. I also need to participate in certain activities, which themselves have a meaning for me, because of the purposes which I have in life. And I need to *share* those purposes with other human beings – to belong to a culture in which these purposes have a place, so that others mean the same by 'computer screen' that I do. The end result of the learning is that I not only discriminate between computer screens and other objects with similar properties, but know and can say *why* I make that discrimination in the way I do, and in the way that others with the same concept do.

All that is part of what is meant by being a subject of perception, as opposed to an object which merely passively responds to stimuli: subjects are in part *active* in response to what they see, and know *why* they are active in the way they are. Thus, materialism in the sense just described is just as incoherent as dualism. Contrary to dualism, the perceiving subject is not some 'inner' entity, but something which by its very nature 'opens out on to' the world. But contrary to materialism, perception requires subjectivity. Perceiving cannot be just an ordinary causal relation between objects in the world, any more than it can be a relation between a subject outside the world and objects inside. It must involve both a subject and an object, but the subject must be in some sense 'inside' the world. How that is possible will be explored in the next section.

THE BODY AS SUBJECT

The subject who perceives must be situated within the world – must be located at a particular place at a particular time. A perceiver experiences the world, as said earlier, from a certain perspective or point of view. To be within the world is to be an object, and, like all the other things within the world, a *physical* or *material* object. Not all kinds of physical object can sensibly be said to 'perceive', however, only those which are equipped with sense organs of various kinds which respond in certain ways to certain kinds of stimuli – light, sounds, and so on – reaching them from objects around them. Objects with sense organs are biological organisms, or living bodies. So perceivers are necessarily biological objects. Biological organisms are 'in' the world, not only in the literal sense of being located in a certain place at a certain time, but in the sense that they make *demands* on other objects in the world, and so have connections with them other than relations in space and time and causal relationships. A living being, as such, has certain needs – for food, drink, air to breathe, sexual activity, protection from excessive heat and cold, and so on, which create demands on the surrounding environment – for things that will satisfy them. If this is true of perceivers in general, it must clearly be true of ourselves as perceivers. We too are a particular kind of object in the world, namely, a certain species of biological organisms; and our links with our environment are in part created by the demands resulting from our biological needs.

How does this differ from the kind of materialism briefly described in the previous section? As far as it goes, it does not differ at all. The materialist form of objectivism treats perceivers (human beings) as just one kind of object in the world. An object, Merleau-Ponty says, can be defined as something which can be divided into a number of separate parts, and which has only external and mechanical relationships between these parts, or between itself and other objects (2002: 84). This is how scientific biology, within the objectivist framework, regards human and other organic bodies. They are complex physicochemical systems, whose behaviour can ultimately be reduced to the physical movements of matter in space, or the chemical transformations of substances. All these biological processes are regarded scientifically as special cases of the kinds of physical and chemical processes which occur in the world generally, and so as ultimately governed by the same laws as them.

Scientific objectivism sees biological organisms, then, as objects, in other words 'from the outside', from a detached point of view. But, Merleau-Ponty asks, can we regard our own biological existence in that detached way? The biological needs which create demands on my world are *my* needs, needs which I feel 'from the inside', not just observe 'from the outside'. Hunger, in my own case, is not something which I coolly and dispassionately observe, but something which I feel, and which gives a certain meaning to the objects I observe – some of them, like a loaf of bread, will satisfy my hunger, or at least alleviate it, others, like a stone, will not. And my body is in other ways something which I live from the inside, rather than just observe. The movements of my body from place to place are *my* movements, done to achieve some purpose of my own (say, to visit a certain place, or to go for a walk and so get some fresh air): I experience them as part of my life, and do not observe them in the detached way I might observe, say, the movements of billiard balls across the table when I am not playing billiards. When I raise my arm, I experience this movement of a piece of matter as 'my raising my arm', something I do for some purpose of my own – to vote in a show of hands, or to ask permission to leave the room, or to greet a friend, or maybe simply to get a bit of exercise. The movements of my whole body, and of different parts of it, have a meaning for me. I make them for a reason, and I know what that reason is, without having to accumulate empirical evidence. When something sharp cuts through my skin, I *feel pain*: the cutting is not just an observable fact affecting some object, but something which forms part of my experience, my life. Or again, when I see something funny happening, I *feel* amused, and can tell others why I do, without the need to formulate and test any explanatory hypothesis.

For these reasons, my embodied behaviour neither needs explanation in terms of laws of physics and chemistry, nor can it be explained adequately in these ways. If you ask me why I am going for a walk, the answer cannot be found in physics and chemistry, though physics and chemistry might explain the way in which 'instructions' are transmitted from my brain to the muscles in my leg and cause them to move in the way we call 'walking'. I myself can tell you, even without any knowledge of physics, chemistry, or physiology, why I'm going for a walk – it's because I've been indoors working all day and feel the need for some fresh air and relaxation. Of course, I can only satisfy that need in this way because I have a brain and nervous system and functioning legs, but it does not follow that those facts about me explain why I am doing what I am doing.

Much the same could be said about the example of raising my arm. To describe the physiological processes involved in raising someone's arm will not explain why I raised my arm on this particular occasion, unless it was some kind of purely automatic response – a type of reflex. For that, we need to give my reasons for doing so. And to explain why I am smiling, it will not be enough to describe any brain mechanisms which may be involved in feeling amusement, *unless* the feeling of amusement had been produced by, for example, an experimenter stimulating the appropriate areas of my brain from the outside. Except in those very exceptional circumstances, I should need to say what it was about the situation that I found funny. Interestingly, when the kind of experiment just referred to is carried out, the experimental subjects usually try to rationalize their amusement by finding something – indeed anything – in their situation which they can plausibly give as a reason for their feelings. This is sometimes interpreted to mean that even in normal cases, the 'reasons' we give are just rationalizations. But that seems merely perverse: it seems far more likely that the rationalizations in the experimental cases are attempts to fit them into the more normal pattern which holds when we have genuine reasons for feeling amused, or whatever. (For more on Merleau-Ponty's views on the explanation of behaviour, see Chapter 4.)

So we human beings are both objects and subjects. We are essentially embodied, and in a sense are to be identified with our bodies – we could not be part of the world unless we were bodily creatures, and in that way objects just like any other. As objects, we are responsive, just like other objects, to the influences that things around us exert. We are governed by the self-same laws of physics and chemistry as anything else in the universe. Nothing that happens to us cannot be explained, from one point of view, by those laws. Even our biological processes can be explained from that point of view ultimately in physico-chemical terms. So far, Merleau-Ponty's view is as materialistic as anyone's in the history of philosophy. Where he begins to diverge from certain traditional forms of materialism is in his claim that the 'point of view' just mentioned is not the only, or the most fundamental, way of looking at human beings.

Even as biological creatures, human beings cannot be treated as nothing but mechanistic, physico-chemical systems. Living organisms are centres of *activity* in the world. To be alive is to respond to the world, not merely passively, in the way something non-living, like a heap of soil, does, but in a more active, internally directed, way. A heap of soil is affected from the outside by wind, rain and other physical forces: they change its shape, its size and many other properties. A living organism, of course, is also affected in these ways: if I lie in the sun for long enough, my skin turns brown, whether I want it to or not. But, as a living organism, I also initiate actions on the surrounding environment: I have certain needs and desires of my own which lead me to act in certain ways – for instance, I may take a spade and re-arrange the pile of soil because it is blocking the path to my house and so causing inconvenience to me and to my visitors. The fact, if it is a fact, that my having these needs and desires can be explained, at least in part, by science – by natural selection, say, or by biochemistry, or both – is not incompatible with saying that they are internal initiators of the things I do. They are still my needs and desires, no matter how it came about that I have them.

So there is another way of regarding human beings (or other creatures) as biological organisms: as well as seeing them as physicochemical systems, responding to external influences, we can also see them as internally directed living beings, who act on the world around them. To say this is to say that they are *subjects* as well as objects: they are embodied, but they are embodied subjects. Both the words in this phrase are equally important. Human subjectivity necessarily expresses itself through the human body: quite simply, I see with my eyes, hear with my eyes, act through moving my arms and legs, speak through moving my vocal chords, smile through arranging my face in the relevant way, and so on. I could not have any subjective response to the world unless I had a body, and I could not have typically human subjective responses unless I had a typically human body. At the same time, my body is not a mere object in the world, as it is both for Cartesian dualists and traditional materialists, but something I 'live', something I inhabit, as the vehicle of my subjective experience. It is as true to say that my body is me as that I am my body.

The subjective view of one's own body must be primary. I must have experience of the world before I can begin to develop knowledge of it and so develop a conception of an objective world, independent of my experience of it – a world which is not mine, but the common world of all experiencers. Science is, of course, the most important part of our knowledge of the world, since it is what we achieve when we seek only *knowledge* of the world, unmixed with our own personal interests, values and aspirations. Scientific knowledge includes biology, the science of living bodies, one example of which is human beings as living creatures. But we have to *live* our bodies as vehicles of our subjective experience of the world, which is shaped by our interests and values, before we can consider those same bodies as objects of scientific study, disinterestedly and dispassionately.

This distinction between the lived body of our experience and the objective body of science is not Cartesian dualism: these are not two bodies or two separate things, but the same body described from different points of view. We can consider a simple example. My desire to eat this apple is, from the subjective part of view, something which I experience, more or less intensely. It is something which is more or less important to me than other aspects of my experience, such as my desire to get on with working on this chapter. It can motivate me to act in various ways – most obviously to reach out and eat the apple, but also in other ways, such as to write a poem about apples. And the appropriate explanation for my having this desire must include some reference to my personal values (not necessarily shared with others) – my taste in apples, or in food generally, my present feelings of hunger, my hedonistic love of such sensual pleasures as eating apples, and so forth. But the same desire can also be looked at objectively, and so without reference to any personal values of my own. I, like all human beings, feel hunger because the human body is so structured that it needs to derive energy from eating food. I can feel pleasure in eating apples because I have tastebuds which respond to chemicals in apples; these feelings motivate a desire to eat an apple because of certain chemical connections between the processes in the brain and nervous system involved in having the feelings and those involved in desiring to eat.

We cannot have desires (or thoughts, feelings, wishes, hopes, etc.) without a brain and nervous system which function in certain ways described by the biological sciences. In this sense, our subjectivity is as it is because we are embodied, biological, creatures of a certain kind: the biological structures common to human beings are the general condition for the possibility of having a mental life of the kind we have. It explains that mental life in that it provides these general conditions of possibility. But it is not what we describe when we talk about our experience, and does not replace what we describe. If asked to describe my present state of mind, I should speak, not of my brain states, but of my feelings and desires. If asked to explain my desire for the apple, I should speak, not of the chemical preconditions of my present brain states, but of my reasons for feeling this way. Human beings are embodied *subjects*; however, their subjectivity is not something merely *attached* to their bodies, but something which is inconceivable without a body of a particular form.

Merleau-Ponty's insistence on the embodiment of human subjectivity also implies something important about intentionality. More will be said about this in the next chapter, but for the moment let us say only this. Brentano, Husserl and many other philosophers have associated intentionality exclusively with *consciousness* – with our conscious directedness to things outside ourselves. My desire is *for* an apple: I can consciously identify the intentional object of my desire – if someone asks me what I want, I can say without hesitation, 'An apple'. But if subjectivity is essentially embodied, then it becomes at least conceivable that intentional directedness need not be explicitly conscious in that sense. It becomes a *biological* feature, a feature of things insofar as they are living, rather than insofar as they are capable of conscious thought. Perhaps non-human living things might also be subjects, possessors of intentionality. (This leaves open the possibility, which we shall explore further later, that conscious intentionality may be particularly attributed to human beings, and may have important special characteristics.)

This is in fact Merleau-Ponty's view. Subjectivity and intentionality are not, for him, confined to the human species, and even human intentionality does not belong to us by virtue of our consciousness alone, but by virtue of our being living beings who are not always explicitly conscious of what they are aiming for. In Part One, Chapter 1 of *Phenomenology of Perception*, Merleau-Ponty takes the example of an insect which has lost one leg (2002: 90). In performing an instinctive action involving its legs, the insect will substitute a sound leg for the missing one. This substitution, he argues, is neither the result of an automatic mechanism set up in advance (something, as we should now say, 'programmed' into the insect's patterns of behaviour), nor, of course, is it a conscious adoption of a means to achieve its (equally conscious) aim. Neither of these explanations really shows why it does not behave in the same way when the leg is not amputated, but merely tied so that it cannot be used. Rather, if we want to understand what the insect does, we should see it as having a 'world' in the same sense that we do. The objects round about it, and its own body in relation to them, have a 'meaning' for it: it has what Merleau-Ponty calls its own 'scheme of things' – its legs, for instance, are for it ways of achieving certain of its aims (say, to remove an obstacle in its path). The limb which is merely tied, because it is still part of its body, still counts in its scheme of things: as Merleau-Ponty puts it, 'the current of activity which flows towards the world still passes through it' (ibid.).

To 'have a world' is to see the objects around one as having a meaning for oneself, not simply as objects with physical and spatial relationships to oneself considered as simply another object. The apple is for me not merely an object of a certain shape and size a metre away from my eyes, but *something to eat and to enjoy*. This is the sense in which the soil in front of the insect is part of the world which the insect's aims construct – because it is, from the insect's point of view, an obstacle in its path. It is thus the intentional object of the insect's thoughts, because we cannot explain the insect's behaviour in relation to it otherwise. The insect is solving a problem which confronts it. But to say it is the intentional object of the insect's thoughts manifestly does not mean that the insect consciously says to itself,'Here is something in my way which I must remove if I am to get any further'. Intentionality is therefore not confined to conscious thoughts, desires, wishes, hopes, etc.

Merleau-Ponty contrasts this kind of animal or biological behaviour with the purely mechanical response to a situation found, for example, when a drop of oil moves in accordance with the external forces which are acting on it. The drop of oil could be seen metaphorically as 'solving a problem which confronts it', but that is *only* a metaphor. Its situation can be entirely described in external or objective terms: it is in a certain place, with certain relations to other objects, which impede or facilitate its movements in various ways, and its movements can be explained entirely in terms of general physical laws and its relations to other objects. For instance, it flows down one way rather than another because there are obstacles in its path in the latter direction. It has no *view* of the situation, so that its own view does not enter into the description of what the situation is. Even such a simple organism as an instinct, however, necessarily has a view of its situation, because it has certain *needs* of its own. The insect with the missing leg therefore *literally* 'faces a problem', defined, not just in terms of external features, but of its own internal needs. It needs to progress, and something is an obstacle to its satisfying that need, so it must adapt its functioning in order to solve that problem. We can't explain what happens without taking into account its felt needs as well as the external features of the situation.

Thus, to talk about intentionality or subjectivity is to talk about a certain way of explaining behaviour, in terms of internal features of the behaver's being which are essentially directed towards certain objects and in terms of which those objects have a certain meaning for the behaver. Sometimes, especially in human beings, who have a language in which to formulate it, this meaning will be explicitly conscious: the being in question will be able to say immediately what the meaning is. But even in human beings the meaning is not necessarily made explicit in this way. Merleau-Ponty gives many examples, especially from pathological or abnormal types of human behaviour. For instance, he discusses in several passages the well-known phenomenon of the 'phantom limb' (see Merleau-Ponty 2002: 87ff.). When someone has lost a limb, as a result of accident or surgery, they sometimes still have the illusion of feelings in the missing limb: someone who has lost their left leg may perhaps still seem to themselves to feel pain in the left big toe. How are we to explain this strange phenomenon? Working within the objectivist framework, we might be inclined to offer a physiological explanation. One kind of physiological explanation might be that the nerve path from where the leg had been to the brain still exists, even though it is much shorter now. So a stimulus applied to the stump of the leg would send the same kind of 'message' to the appropriate centre in the brain as would have been sent from the leg itself previously. The brain would thus still have the idea of a leg. This would be a 'central' theory: the phantom limb would in effect be a collection of processes in the brain. The central theory might be reinforced by the fact that, apparently, there are some cases of brain injury in which the injured person has not in fact lost a limb, but still experiences the 'phantom limb' phenomenon.

But identifying phantom limbs with a collection of brain processes fails to explain other aspects of the phenomenon: for instance, the fact that an imaginary limb feels to be enormous immediately following the operation, but shrinks as the patient comes to accept his mutilation. This kind of case, Merleau-Ponty suggests, calls for a more 'psychological' explanation – that people's sense of having a phantom limb is a way of dealing with the emotional problem of the loss of a part of themselves. The person imagines a phantom limb because he or she is unwilling to accept emotionally the loss of the functions which he or she used to perform with that limb. Their world, in the sense of the world *as they see* it and as they live in it has changed, and this creates a problem for them. But of course to say that they conjure up a phantom limb as a way of solving an emotional problem is not to say that they *consciously* or *deliberately* do so: their illusion may have a purpose for them without their being aware of what that purpose is.

To be an embodied subject, then, is to be an active being, with needs which motivate actions and in relation to which elements in the surrounding environment are meaningful. It is to be in a world which is in this way partly a world of one's own: one does not create the things in the world in the sense of bringing them into existence, but one's needs and thoughts about the world, rooted in one's nature as a biological organism, give a unity of meaning to those objects, which makes them into a single world. At the same time, to be embodied means that living in the world comes before *conscious* thought about the world: experience is 'pre-reflective' at base, and reflection concerns what is pre-reflectively given. In the next chapter, we shall explore further what this means for our understanding of human and animal behaviour.

CHAPTER 4

BEHAVIOUR

REDUCTIONISM

As has been said already, the task of phenomenology is to enable us to see things in a new way, by taking us back to the roots of our present ways of seeing. In many ways, though not all, this is like the later Wittgenstein's conception of philosophy. Wittgenstein held that we are held captive by certain pictures – visions of what things *must* be like. We have a natural tendency to over-simplify the complexity of things, in the interest of having a coherent picture of reality. For instance, we seek a general 'theory of meaning', an account of what it is for a word or other expression to 'mean' something, of what *the* relation is between 'language' and 'reality'. What we need to remind ourselves of is that there are *many different* ways in which language 'connects up with' reality, corresponding to the many different ways in which we use language. Other general 'pictures', according to Wittgenstein, captivate us because of this picture of how language works: we neglect the differences between the ways in which we actually use an expression in different contexts, and so end up assimilating its meaning in one context to its meaning in another. For example, because to say, 'I know that earth is an oblate spheroid' implies that I have an assurance of this fact based on evidence, we assume that that must be true also of 'I know that I am in pain', and invent a faculty of 'introspection' as the source of the evidence on which we rely in the second case. The job of Wittgenstein's kind of philosophy is to free us from these distorting pictures by reminding us of the different ways in which we use language.

Phenomenology, on Merleau-Ponty's interpretation, has a similarly liberating role. The picture which holds us captive in this case, however, is not generated by neglect of the ways in which we use language, but by neglect of what our ordinary, pre-reflective experience of reality tells us. We neglect that pre-reflective experience in favour of certain theories about reality which have been developed, on the basis of experience, in order to explain how that experience is possible. The theory which aims to explain experience is substituted for a description of experience itself: we come to think that the theoretical description gets us closer to the heart of what reality is actually like than our pre-reflective contact with it can ever do. This is the illusion from which the phenomenologist seeks to free us – not, as was said earlier, in order to denigrate the theoretical account, but in order to make clear what its proper place is in our thinking.

One crucial way in which such a picture holds us captive is in relation to human behaviour and the ways in which we can understand it. We began to consider the understanding of human behaviour in the last chapter, but we should now expand on that discussion in more detail. Human beings, as was said in the last chapter, are, Merleau-Ponty argues, essentially *biological* creatures, living organisms of a particular species and therefore having certain physiological structures. The study of life in the modern world is, like that of other aspects of reality, a part of science, conducted within the general theoretical framework of science. In biological science, as in other branches of study, we seek to understand how the relevant phenomena come to be as they are. We formulate hypotheses about what causes what, and test these hypotheses against empirical data, to see which hypotheses are confirmed and can be accepted and which are falsified and must be rejected. This testing is a job for the whole scientific community: no one scientist, however distinguished, is to be regarded as an authority such that what he or she says ought to be accepted just because he or she says it. Instead, any scientist's hypotheses have to be tested by others. The original experiments or observations which that scientist believed to confirm the hypothesis have to be repeatable by others, and it is only if they are so repeatable, and if no other experiments or observations falsify the hypothesis, that it comes to be accepted as something more than a hypothesis – as a generally accepted 'causal law' of the science.

In scientific biology, this means that nothing can be accepted as a causal law unless it applies to the relevant organisms in general, not just to the particular organisms studied by the originator of the hypothesis. In human biology, it is possible that a scientist may first be struck by something about his or her own body, and may formulate a hypothesis on that basis. But such a hypothesis can come to be accepted as a law of biology only if it applies equally to other bodies. From the point of view of scientific biology, human bodies have to be looked upon from the outside, in a way which is indifferent to *whose* body it happens to be. Any scientific explanation of human biological processes must be *general* in form: it must explain how one body works by reference to how all bodies of the relevant kind work. And this must obviously mean that, if I am a scientific biologist, I must explain how my own body works in terms of general principles affecting all human bodies of my type. If, for instance, I have high blood pressure, then the explanation must be in terms of general causes of this condition, which apply equally to other human beings (indeed other non-human animals) as to me. In that sense, I must look on my own body 'from the outside', as if it were nothing special, just one instance of a general kind of objects in the world.

This external or objective view of living organisms is not only one possible and perfectly valid way of looking at them, it is one which is essential for certain very important human purposes. If we are to practise medicine, for instance, we seek to alleviate human suffering and disability by changing the state of the bodily organs involved. Suppose a doctor is treating someone with diabetes. Successful treatment depends on knowledge of what the general causes of diabetes are, so that some means can be found of controlling those causes, and so alleviating the suffering which results from them. Finding out the general causes of diabetes involves treating diabetes as an objective process in a living organism, which has equally objective preconditions – preceding states of the organism which result in this process. The objectivity required in this approach would be hopelessly compromised if we were preoccupied with the purely individual features of this person's diabetes, such as what it meant to her to be diabetic. Even if a doctor were treating her own diabetes, she would have to get outside, as far as possible, her own subjective views on it and look on it as just another case of this human condition.

The great successes of a science-based medicine are one reason why the scientific or objective way of looking at living organisms has such prestige in modern culture. But once this prestige is established, its connection with some of the human purposes behind thinking in this way tends to be forgotten. The scientific view comes to be seen as self-evidently more correct and rational than any other. Here we come back to human and other animal behaviour. For it tends to be taken as read in the modern world that scientific, or objectivist, ways of explaining human behaviour must be preferable to any other. This way of thinking first of all defines human behaviour as just another example of the behaviour of an object. To use again the example given in the previous chapter (and taken from Merleau-Ponty), the movement of a trickle of oil across a surface can be described as the 'behaviour' of the oil. The oil, let us say, is spilled from a bottle onto a crumpled sheet of paper lying on a sloping surface. It moves down the slope following the course allowed for it by the crumples in the surface of the paper. Its 'behaviour' consists in its movement through space along a certain course and in a certain direction.

In our ordinary, pre-scientific, way of thinking about much of human behaviour (what some philosophers, as we have seen, call 'folk psychology'), we think that there are important differences between what human beings do and what such things as trickles of oil 'do'. Indeed, the very need which I felt there to put inverted commas round the second occurrence of the word 'do' indicates that we don't normally think that inanimate objects like oil slicks 'do' anything at all – things just happen to them, caused by things outside them. To say that human beings 'do' things is to imply that they have some *purpose* in doing them, that the behaviour is, as it were, internally directed rather than externally caused. For instance, if I walk along a road in a certain direction, my movements are not, on this way of thinking, simply responses to external stimuli, but expressions of my purpose in walking to a certain place: I want to get there, and I believe that this is a good way to do so, and that is why I am moving as I am. None of this obviously applies to the oil-slick's movements across the paper.

But precisely this is what some philosophers and scientists object to in 'folk psychology'. Calling it 'folk' psychology is meant as an insult: it implies that it is a quaint and rather old-fashioned survival, not really fitting a modern scientific way of thinking about human behaviour, rather in the way that 'folk-medicine' is supposed to be superseded by modern scientific treatments. Merleau-Ponty refers to this objection at the beginning of his first published book *The Structure of Behaviour*:

Grasped from the inside, my behavior appears as directed, as gifted with an intention and a meaning. Science seems to demand that we reject these characteristics as appearances under which a reality of another kind must be discovered. (Merleau-Ponty 1965: 7)

Instead of talking about 'direction', 'intention' and 'meaning', the objectors say, we should use only the kind of vocabulary in describing and explaining human behaviour that we would use in talking about oil-slicks. (Or else, if we must use the 'direction' vocabulary, we must be able at least to 'translate' it into the other kind of language.)

As Merleau-Ponty makes clear here, the objection to folk-psychology is essentially that it makes use of concepts which have to be 'grasped from the inside'. If we explain someone's anger, for instance, by saying, 'He's angry because he feels that he has not been taken seriously', we use the concept of a 'feeling', which is thought of as something which can only be directly accessed by the person himself. (As we shall see later, Merleau-Ponty would question this assumption about thoughts, feelings, etc.) But if that is so, then feelings and other such things cannot be studied scientifically: science is concerned only with what is *publicly* observable, that is, with what can be observed by anyone at all. Still following this line of thought, we come to think that a *scientific* explanation of human behaviour must use only concepts of entities which can be publicly observed, which are 'objective' in that sense. So science rejects folk-psychology as merely a pre-scientific illusion, based on a belief in mysterious 'hidden' entities, which cannot be observed from the outside: the real truth about human behaviour, as about anything else, must be revealed by objective science.

There are two main ways in which such an objective science of human behaviour has historically been pursued. One is what is usually called 'behaviourism'. The folk-psychological talk of 'inner entities', like thoughts, feelings, meanings, consciousness and so on, must, according to behaviourists, be replaced by talk about outward behaviour, which we can observe. For example, instead of talking about his feeling of anger, which is 'inside' him and which he alone has direct access to, we should talk about his flushed cheeks, his waving arms, his loud exclamations, which we can all see and hear.

Equally, the causes of these phenomena must be publicly observable: it must be that an external 'stimulus', acting on the senses, causes a 'response' in the person, in the form of the movements which we observe. Sometimes, the connection between stimulus and response may be innate, 'hard-wired' as it were into the person's brain and nervous system: an example might be a simple reflex, like the knee-jerk reflex. But in the case of human beings, and especially in the case of the more complex forms of behaviour, the stimulus–response connection is *learned*. The founder of behaviourism as a school of psychology, John Watson (1878–1958), was very much impressed by the ideas of the Russian physiologist Ivan Pavlov (1849–1936) about what he called 'conditioned reflexes'. Probably the best-known example of a conditioned reflex is that of dogs who came to salivate when a bell was rung. Initially, the dogs salivated naturally when food was presented to them, but a bell was invariably rung at the same time as the presentation of the food. In time, the dogs came to salivate when the bell was rung, even when there was no food around. Their 'salivation reflex' had been 'conditioned' by association to be a response to this new stimulus.

The dogs, one might say, had 'learned' to regard the ringing of the bell as a stimulus, but there was no intellectual or inner activity involved in this 'learning', only a constant association of stimulus with response. Human learning, according to the behaviourists, could be treated as a more complex version of this kind of conditioning. So we could account for much of human behaviour without bringing in processes 'grasped from the inside', relying only on associations that we could observe from the outside. For example, we could replace talk of someone's refusing to do something because she thought it was wrong by talk about her being conditioned by painful stimuli (punishment) to refrain from the kinds of actions with which that stimulus had become associated.

One problem with behaviourism, even from the objectivist point of view, is that it does not seem possible to identify thoughts *only* with externally observable movements of the body. Consider a person who is angry – for a behaviourist, to say this is equivalent to saying that the person's outward facial expression and 'verbal behaviour' are of an appropriate kind: her face is flushed, she is waving her arms about and shouting loudly. But that does not seem to distinguish anger from other cases in which the outward behaviour would be the same: her face might be flushed because she suffers from high blood pressure, she might be waving her hands and shouting in distress rather than anger. Surely, we might feel, there must be something going on 'behind the scenes' to distinguish behaviour which is (as we say) an 'expression' of anger from that which 'expresses' other emotions, such as distress. Moreover, we can all recognize that often people can be said to feel anger (or distress, or any other emotion, not to mention having thoughts, wishes, and so on) which are not expressed at all in outward behaviour. But if we are to stick to our objectivist approach, even this 'behind the scenes' activity must be in principle observable by anyone. The obvious candidate which suggests itself is processes going on in the nervous system and brain of the person in question. These things are not normally observable in everyday life, but there is no reason why they cannot be revealed in principle, using modern methods of studying human neurophysiology.

So this gives us a different kind of objectivist approach, which accepts the importance of something 'inner', but locates that something *literally* inside the behaving person, that is, literally underneath the skin, and so can be objectively or scientifically studied. Whereas behaviourism equates thoughts, feelings and so on with external behaviour, this approach takes account of the processes in the brain and nervous system which are causally responsible for that external behaviour. In the most radical version of this view, usually called 'eliminative materialism', it is suggested that we need to get rid of such 'folk-psychological' terms as 'anger', 'distress', 'thought', 'feeling' and so on and replace them with terms drawn from neuroscience, like 'neuron-firing'. Thus, instead of saying that someone was angry because they felt insulted by someone else's remarks, we should say, if we are to be truly scientific, something along the lines of 'they behaved aggressively to someone else because certain centres in their brain were active in certain ways'.

In *The Structure of Behaviour*, Merleau-Ponty seeks to show that both these types of objectivist approach are inadequate even from a scientific point of view. His argument there takes the form of an analysis of the work of physiologists and psychologists themselves. Most of his discussion focuses on behaviourism and conditioned-reflex theory, but the points which he makes can be applied equally to the neuroscientific approach just outlined. We'll begin by considering his remarks about behaviourism, and then move on to neuroscience later. The very notion of a 'response' to a 'stimulus', if it is to be of any practical use, he argues, requires us to use the ideas of 'meaning' and 'intention' which the behaviourists were seeking to eliminate. So does the notion of 'conditioning'. Consider again the example given earlier: the 'painfulness' of the kind of stimulus we call 'punishment' is not a physical feature of what is done (a slap on the wrist, for instance). It is a meaning attributed to it by the person receiving it. Equally, the 'conditioning' will only lead to inhibition of the desire to do something wrong if the person being conditioned *sees* the relevant action as wrong. Suppose a child is spanked every time she tells a lie. The end result may well be that she feels inhibited in later life from telling lies. But this conditioning will work only if she understands the spanking as a *punishment*, intended to make her stop doing what she is doing, and that what she is being spanked for is *telling a lie*, rather than, say, for uttering words. The association between stimulus and response is one between the *meaning* of both for the person whose behaviour is allegedly being 'conditioned', and in that sense is 'subjective'.

In the cases of the knee-jerk reflex, or the dogs' salivation, the 'behaviour' in question is indeed simply a matter of physical movements, which can be entirely described in objective terms. But in more complex cases, in human beings or indeed in other animals, we cannot, Merleau-Ponty would argue, define behaviour as a 'series of physical events', but rather as 'the projection outside the organism of a *possibility* which is internal to it' (1965: 125). Behaviour is a way of treating the world, where the 'world' means the world *for* the person who is behaving, the world as having a certain meaning for the person. It is 'intentional', in the sense described in Chapter 1: namely, in being *directed towards* a certain intentional object. That is, we can only properly speak of behaviour (at least of these more complex kinds) if we regard the physical movements as not caused by something external to the person engaged in the behaviour, but motivated by a subjective or inner meaning arising from the person's own internal view of the world. To behave angrily, for instance, is to express anger *about* what someone is believed to have done or something which has happened, seen under a certain description (as 'insulting' or 'unfair' or 'hostile' or whatever). What is wrong with behaviourism, on this argument, is thus that it tries to operate with an inadequate notion of what is meant by 'behaviour'.

A very similar critique could be offered of the neuroscientific approach. To equate being angry (to use the same example again) with physical processes in the brain and nervous system caused by other physical processes is to ignore the intentional nature of anger. A series of neuron firings in the brain only has any connection with anger if the person in whose brain they occur sees the situation as warranting anger on his or her part. The fact that these firings were preceded by other neurological processes may be a causal explanation of the firings, but does not begin to explain why the person felt anger: because of its intentional character, the explanation of anger has to be in terms of the angry person's way of regarding his or her experience. It is somewhat like the case of a car: the workings of the engine might explain why the car moves at the speed it does, but cannot explain the *direction* of the car's movement towards its destination. That can be explained only in terms of the driver's thoughts and desires, which in turn can be explained only by her reasons for thinking or desiring in that way. 'Why is your car able to move at all?' 'Because it has a functioning engine' – that is a causal explanation. 'Why are you driving to Aberdeen at that speed?' 'Because I want to do some shopping there' – that is a reason explanation, in terms of the meaning I find in my present situation, and which then links together my various physical movements – my hands controlling the steering wheel, my feet operating the pedals. The functioning of the car-engine clearly could not explain why it is moving towards Aberdeen, rather than towards Dundee or Edinburgh or anywhere else. Equally, the factors which cause my brain cells to operate in the way they do when I am angry cannot explain why I am angry, rather than distressed, or afraid, or happy.

AGAINST 'CAUSAL THINKING'

But is this talk of 'subjective meaning' just reintroducing the hidden 'inner world', which both behaviourists and advocates of the neuroscientific approach were attempting to get rid of in the interests of a truly scientific account of the things people do? Merleau-Ponty would say, 'No'. In his radio talks referred to earlier, published in book form as *The World of Perception*, he uses the same example of anger which we have used above to make this point. He imagines someone being annoyed with him, and expressing his anger by aggressive gestures and shouting. He asks where this anger is. Is it 'in the person's mind', that is, in some hidden place 'behind the scenes', distinct from anything physical? But what can that mean? Can we really imagine the feeling apart from the outward actions and gestures which can be observed? The anger is 'in the room': 'It is in the space between him and me that it unfolds' (Merleau-Ponty 2004: 83). It is on the man's face, though not in the way his tears are. Rather, it is the *meaning* which the man's facial expressions and shouting have, both for the observer and for the man himself. What it means to be angry can not be stated otherwise than by including the typical behavioural expressions of anger (and of course the generally accepted intelligible reasons for being angry). These meanings are not located in some internal world of mind: they exist 'in the space between people'. The behaviourists were not wrong to equate thought, feeling and so on with 'behaviour': where they went astray, as was said earlier, was in their conception of what that meant, their idea that 'behaviour' simply referred to a sequence of physical movements. Being angry is behaving in certain ways which have the meaning 'anger', and this meaning is as publicly observable, and so as suitable for scientific study, as the loud sound of the angry person's voice.

Similarly, Merleau-Ponty would argue, it is not wrong to think that being angry, or being in any mental state at all, necessarily involves, for beings like us, certain processes taking place in the brain and nervous system. We are, as we saw in the last chapter, essentially embodied beings. The kind of bodies we have, including the kinds of brains and nervous systems we have, make possible the kinds of thoughts and emotions we have. Mental disturbances, for instance, cannot be defined either as purely 'psychic' (or mental) or as purely 'somatic' (bodily), but as both. From the 'somatic' point of view, there is an organic accident – something has happened to the body, probably to the brain or nervous system, and the disturbance can be regarded as a 'commentary', to use Merleau-Ponty's word, on this accident. From the 'psychic' point of view, the disturbance is a matter of the human significance of the bodily event. But this is a matter of the direction of emphasis, not a distinction between two separate types of events – in Cartesian terms, between a 'material' event and a 'mental' one (see Merleau-Ponty 2002: 102).

The fault which both behaviourists and advocates of the neuro-scientific approach have in common is a mistake about what the *explanation* of our thoughts and feelings involves. Both are guilty of what Merleau-Ponty calls 'causal thinking'. They assume that the only rationally acceptable way of explaining anything, including human behaviour, is that adopted by the sciences, and that there is only one form of explanation which can be called truly 'scientific', because it alone is genuinely objective. The mainstream view in the philosophy of science has long been that scientific explanation must have a particular logical form, sometimes called the 'deductive-nomological' (DN) form, sometimes the 'covering law model'. Both of these terms refer to essentially the same pattern of explanation. To explain some particular thing which happens, according to this theory, is to show it as an instance or example of a general causal law. Logically, the explanation must have the following form: 'Whenever A occurs, then B occurs' (law-statement); A has occurred (statement of 'specific initial conditions'); therefore B has occurred (conclusion: statement of event to be explained). This is a logically valid form of argument, so if the premises are both true, we can validly infer the conclusion, and can legitimately say that 'A caused B' or that the occurrence of B has been causally explained.

A simple example may make the point clearer. It is a true generalization that, at sea-level, water heated to 100 degrees Celsius boils. We can validly infer from that generalization, plus the premise 'This water was heated to 100 degrees at sea-level' the conclusion 'Therefore this water boiled'. We can also express this by saying that it was heating the water to 100 degrees that *caused* it to boil, or conversely that the boiling of the water was to be explained by the fact that it was heated to 100 degrees. If we change the tense of the verbs, we could use this same pattern of reasoning as the basis for a prediction: 'Whenever water is heated at sea-level to 100 degrees, it will boil; this water has been heated to 100 degrees; therefore it *will* boil.' This illustrates an important point about this kind of explanation: the boiling of the water is explained, or made intelligible, by the heating to 100 degrees, in the sense that it is shown to be *predictable*, or *to be expected*, in those circumstances, given known laws of nature.

The 'causal laws' used in this way in the covering-law model of explanation are *universal empirical generalizations*. That is, they are statements of the form, 'Whenever [an event of type] A occurs, then [an event of type] B occurs', which can be tested against experience. We can test the truth of the generalization about water boiling by seeing whether it works on particular occasions. This account of causal explanation ultimately relies on the analysis of the idea of 'cause' given by the eighteenth-century Scottish philosopher David Hume, who argued that, to say that 'A caused B' on a particular occasion is to say that 'A' and 'B' are distinct events (or, as Merleau-Ponty puts it, 'The object of science is defined by the mutual exteriority of parts and processes' – Merleau-Ponty 1965: 9). Hume also held that, when A is said to cause B, B must have occurred after A, and events of type A must be regularly followed by (or 'constantly conjoined with' to use Hume's terminology) events of type B. We know about the connection between A and B, not by virtue of some kind of rational insight or intuition, but because we have become so used to As being followed by Bs that we have formed the habit of expecting a B when an A occurs. This analysis of scientific explanation appeals to many philosophers and scientists in large part because it seems to make explanation a purely *objective* business. If we ask what it means to 'explain' something, it seems a natural answer to say, 'To explain something is to make it intelligible'. But that answer could be taken to imply that explanation was *subjective*. What is intelligible, after all, is intelligible *to* someone: that is, there must be an individual or individuals who can understand it. For instance, because I speak French, a sentence in French will be intelligible to me, but not to someone who speaks no French at all. But this is clearly no use in science. A scientific explanation cannot be one which works for some people but not for others: it must 'make things intelligible' in a way which doesn't depend on any subjective characteristics of the particular people it is addressed to. For example, people who like chocolate will find no difficulty in understanding why people buy chocolate-bars: it just seems obvious to them that chocolate tastes so good that people will want to buy it. People who loathe the taste of chocolate, on the other hand, will clearly not find that a plausible explanation of its popularity. So it can't be of any scientific value to say, 'People eat chocolate because it tastes so good'. For a scientific explanation, we need a theory which will make it intelligible to anyone, regardless of their personal tastes, in terms of some kind of objective connection between the properties of chocolate and the structure of human taste-buds (which could also be used to explain why some people don't like chocolate at all).

For someone who accepts 'causal thinking', as was said earlier, this pattern of explanation is the only one which a scientific discipline worthy of the name can adopt. Hence, if there is to be (as surely there must be) a science of human behaviour, then it must adopt this way of explaining the things which people do. Human actions must be caused by preceding events which are distinct from them, but constantly conjoined with them in our experience. They must be made intelligible by being shown to be predictable, given the occurrence of their cause. There must be regularities in human behaviour, just as there are in the movements of inanimate objects, and these regularities must be objectively testable. It seems to many people obvious that there are such regularities in human behaviour. In economics, for example, there is the 'law of supply and demand' governing the price which will be charged in a market system for goods: if there is a plentiful supply and not much demand, the price will be lower than if this type of goods is much wanted and in short supply. Constant experience seems to confirm the truth of this. Furthermore, it seems to fit Hume's analysis of causality, in that the 'cause' (the variations in supply and demand) is distinct from the 'effect' (the price of the goods in question) and precedes it – increased supply and decreased demand are followed by a drop in price.

Another plausible-sounding example of a causal explanation of human behaviour can be found in the first chapter of Merleau-Ponty's *The Structure of Behaviour*. Suppose, Merleau-Ponty says, 'I am in a dark room and a luminous spot appears on the wall and moves along it': my eyes follow the movement of the spot. A scientist might explain this by saying that the light is a 'vibratory movement', which acts on my eyes to cause them to move in this way (see Merleau-Ponty 1965: 7). The scientific explanation would presumably be of the covering-law kind: there must be a general law about the effect of light-waves on the retina, and the way in which this causes the eye-muscles to make the eyes turn towards the light. If this law can be shown by empirical testing to be reliable, we have a truly scientific understanding of this phenomenon.

Finally, we could take another, more complex, example, again derived from Merleau-Ponty himself. In several passages, Merleau-Ponty discusses a patient called Schneider, who suffered from a mental disorder which involved, among other things, feelings of detachment from his own body, perceptual problems and sexual disturbances. Merleau-Ponty fully accepts that the root of Schneider's condition was an injury to the occipital region of his brain (see Merleau-Ponty 2002: 130). This could be interpreted in Humean terms as an admission that there is a 'causal connection' between such brain-injuries and the kinds of impairment manifested in Schneider's symptoms. The brain injury can be found to be regularly connected with such impairments, is distinct from them, and precedes them. So we seem here to have a 'psycho-physical law', correlating physical events in the brain with types of behaviour.

These examples, then, seem to show the promise of an objective science of the behaviour of human beings and other animals. This is indeed the route which has been followed by most scientific psychologists and neurophysiologists. Merleau-Ponty, however, wants to argue that, although there are elements of truth in this approach, it is ultimately inadequate. Human behaviour, and indeed the behaviour of other animals, needs to be understood in a different way from that of inanimate objects, or other types of living things, like plants. We have already said a little about this earlier, but we are now in a position to discuss his thesis in more detail. We could begin by looking again at the three examples just given. First, the 'law of supply and demand'. It is true that the correlation of rising and falling prices with variations in supply and demand in a market economy is well-confirmed and familiar to most of us from our everyday experience. But what makes this correlation *explanatory*? Why do we feel that we have understood the rise in the price of gold better when we are told there is an increasing demand for it as a hedge against inflation, but the actual quantities of gold available to meet that demand remain the same? Is it not because we know how people's minds work in a society such as ours, based on a market economy? We know how people's minds in general work, because we know how our own minds work. If we want to protect ourselves against the risk of inflation, one good way to do so is to acquire things which will retain their value in the face of the decline in the value of money: one such thing is gold. So we shall very much want to buy gold. But if there is a limited supply of gold for sale, then we shall have to compete with others who think the same way, and so will have to outbid them – to offer a higher price than them. They will think likewise, so the market value of gold will rise.

In other words, it is not so much our knowledge of the law of supply and demand that enables us to understand the rise in the price of gold, as our understanding of how people, including ourselves, think in a market economy that enables us to see the relevance of the law of supply and demand. We understand that because we are part of a market economy: as such, 'supply', 'demand' and 'price' have connected meanings for us. Variations in price are part of the economic world in which we live, and the price people are prepared to pay for some commodity depends, in that world, on how much they want it and how much of it there is. Contrary to Hume's analysis, price variation is not something distinct from supply-and-demand variation, so that the latter does not cause the former. At the same time, our understanding of the connection depends on our participating in the market economy. Someone who had never been part of such an economic system, and never shared its values, could not begin to understand why the price of gold should go up when a lot of people want it, however well-confirmed it was empirically that there was a constant conjunction between these two things. Secondly, consider the example of my eyes following the moving light in the darkened room. The light which my eyes follow, Merleau-Ponty would argue, is not the light-waves which physics finds acting on my retina, but the light which I actually *perceive*. The 'vibratory movement', he points out, 'is never given to consciousness': I do not see light-waves, I see a spot moving on the wall. Hence, any correlation there may be between the movement of the light (in the physical sense) and the movement of my eyes (considered simply as the movement of two physical objects) has no bearing on understanding why I move my eyes in order to see the spot. Putting it differently, we might say that the causal explanation cannot account for the difference between the movement of a light-sensitive device in response to the movement of a light, and my actively moving my eyes *in order to* follow the light on the wall. In science, Merleau-Ponty points out, we must do without any such ideas as 'in order to', any notions of purpose or intention behind an activity, because they are 'merely subjective' – they 'have no foundation in things and are not intrinsic determinations of them' (Merleau-Ponty 1965: 9). But if we are to adequately account for how things are in the world, then in some kinds of phenomena we need such notions. It was an advance in science when notions of purpose were banished from the study of inanimate nature. People used to explain, for instance, why flowers had such beautiful colours by saying that they were made that way by the Creator for our delight; but that kind of purposive explanation depended on the assumption of a Being with a mind who could have that purpose, and whatever the value of that assumption in other ways it has no place in an empirical science, based only on what we can observe with our senses. When it comes to explaining a human action by the purpose with which human beings perform it, however, then the case for excluding such explanations from empirical science does not seem so convincing. Human beings, after all, can be observed to have purposes, just as they can be observed to have arms, smiles and voices.

The case of Schneider, finally, raises further issues. Merleau-Ponty accepts, as we have seen, that Schneider's brain injury lies at the root of his problems. In this sense, he is accepting that the patient's mental disorders have a causal explanation, based in neurophysiology. But it does not follow that this is all we need in order to gain a proper understanding of his condition (with a view perhaps to offering him psychiatric help). The inability to feel attached, as most of us do, to his own body is a *problem* for Schneider, not because of this causal connection to the damage to his brain, but *in a human sense* – it interferes with his ability to interact normally, and as he would wish, with other human beings. It is when we consider his behaviour as having a human meaning that we need something more than causal explanation. Causal explanation will tell us how it came about that Schneider suffered in this way, but it will not help us to understand what his disorder meant to him, what role it played in his life.

Understanding meaning, as the whole philosophical tradition called 'hermeneutics' would say, is different from causal explanation, as we can see by thinking of the example of understanding the meaning of someone's words, in our own or in a foreign language. Suppose someone says, 'I am afraid'. This involves uttering various sounds, and we can give a causal explanation of their utterance, in terms of the processes which went on in their brain, and the vibrations of their vocal chords, which led to these sounds issuing from their mouth. But this causal account would not tell us what the utterance means – either in the sense of the meaning of these words in English, or in the sense of the experience of fear which these words are used to express. To understand the meaning in the first sense, we need, not knowledge of any causal laws, but knowledge of the English language, which we acquired by using words to mean these things ourselves. To understand the meaning in the second sense, again, we need, not knowledge of causal laws, but an ability to feel fear ourselves, to enter into the experience which is being expressed in the words (or in their equivalents in other languages). In both cases, in other words, understanding depends on being able to share something with the person whose behaviour we are trying to understand, to be able to see the world from their point of view.

This is what objectivists criticize in the idea of this kind of understanding. As said earlier, they regard 'scientific', by which they mean causal, explanation as the only rationally acceptable form of understanding, because it is fully 'objective' – it is the same for everyone, no matter what their point of view. Understanding the human meaning of some behaviour, its meaning for the person who is acting in that way, while it may be important in our social lives together, cannot be part of science, they would say, because it is too 'subjective': it depends too much on being able to put oneself imaginatively in the other person's shoes. Moreover, as they would also say, it does not answer the essential scientific question: why did this person behave in this way, or say these words, or get into this mental condition, at this time and in the way that he or she did? How could we predict that they would do so? When we have understood what his disorder meant for Schneider, they would say, however humanly important that understanding might be, it would still not tell us how people develop the kind of mental disorder he had, or enable us to predict who would be liable to develop it or in what circumstances, or what we can do to prevent them developing it or to cure them of it once they have got it.

In Merleau-Ponty's view, this kind of objectivist criticism only shows that objectivism has missed the point, because it is based on drawing the line between the 'objective' and the 'subjective' at the wrong point. He asks, 'might the opposition between a universe of science – entirely outside of self – and a universe of consciousness – defined by the total presence of self to self – be untenable?' (Merleau-Ponty 1965: 10). The objectivists assume that a scientific study of human behaviour must concern itself only with those publicly observable physical movements which all human behaviour necessarily involves. Because they assume, following the Cartesian tradition, that 'consciousness' (if it exists at all) must be something entirely separate from those physical movements, and something which is hidden away, inaccessible to any human being other than the person whose consciousness it is, they conclude that consciousness cannot play any part in our understanding of human behaviour. If we are to talk about the understanding of the meaning of an action for the person acting, then this inevitably involves reference to consciousness, and so is outside the scope of science.

What this ignores, Merleau-Ponty would say, is that the very phenomenon we are seeking to understand, human behaviour (and perhaps also many aspects of animal behaviour) *cannot be defined* without reference to meaning and consciousness. What is Schneider's condition? Not the way his brain and nervous system function, or not them on their own, but the way in which the functioning of his brain and nervous system have an impact on his life – the meaning which that has for him, and which we can understand only by entering imaginatively into how it appears to his consciousness. The 'objective' phenomenon, in the sense of what we can all observe, is the totality consisting of the brain malfunction resulting from his injury and the consequent disturbed, abnormal, way of behaving and responding to the world which both he and we can see as having a certain meaning. 'Value' and 'signification', Merleau-Ponty suggests, are 'intrinsic determinations of the organism' which are accessible only to this kind of non-causal understanding.

Objectivism about human behaviour is mistaken, because it separates external, physical movements from internal, private consciousness. But human behaviour, Merleau-Ponty argues, is the product of the embodied subjectivity we discussed in the previous chapter. When we see a human being (or other living organism) acting, we do not see a set of mechanical movements, for which we infer some inner mental cause; we see a human being's purpose in his or her movements. This is obvious to us as soon as we free ourselves, as phenomenologists have to, from the presuppositions of objectivism, and consider only what we actually experience. If I asked someone to describe my present behaviour just as they see it, without reference to any scientific theories, they would undoubtedly say, 'You are sitting at your word-processor, writing your book'. What they would not naturally say (unless they wanted to make a philosophical point) is, 'You are sitting in front of an illuminated screen, and your fingers are striking the keys on a keyboard in front of you'. Consciousness, or subjectivity, is not something behind the scenes, hidden from everyone else's view, but is manifested in the movements of my fingers: subjectivity is embodied.

Because my activities express subjectivity (that is: meaning for my consciousness), understanding them necessarily involves understanding that meaning: my actions are like a language, which has to be interpreted. These same physical movements might be involved in writing my tax-return rather than writing this book, or in playing some complicated computer game. To understand *this* action, we need to grasp its specific meaning for me: otherwise, we cannot even begin to understand how it came about that I was sitting here now, doing what I am. But because my subjectivity is essentially *embodied*, I can express this meaning only because my fingers operate in certain ways, and because I have a brain which functions properly to enable me to think about and write about philosophy. These bodily dimensions to my behaviour require to be understood too, and must first be understood in causal terms. And then, in a final twist, we can understand these bodily movements too in terms of their role in expressing the purpose which I have: to write a book on Merleau-Ponty. They too have a meaning, which can be understood.

Living animals of all kinds behave in meaningful ways, because living organisms, as such, have needs and interests, and so purposes for their movements. This applies as much to such simple creatures as insects as to complex animals like apes and human beings. But there is an important difference between human beings and other animals, which leads us to attribute 'consciousness' particularly to humans. Human beings use *language* and other forms of symbolism: they can therefore give explicit expression to the meaning which their actions have for them. This means that the purposes behind human behaviour can be more complex, differentiated and individual. A mouse can have the purpose of seeking food, because it has a biological need for food. But a human being can have non-biological purposes – for example, I may go for a walk because I feel the need for mindless relaxation; and even our biological purposes can be expressed in different ways, determined by culture – for example, I may go to an Italian rather than a Chinese restaurant because I feel the need for Italian rather than Chinese food. This complicated interaction between consciousness, embodiment and culture forms the basis for Merleau-Ponty's account of humanity, which we shall explore in the remaining chapters.

CHAPTER 5

BEING HUMAN

SCIENCE AND HUMANITY

Merleau-Ponty, as has been said before, respects science, as a valid point of view on the world, including ourselves. In his 1948 radio talks, he says:

> If we wish to learn how to prove something, to conduct a thorough investigation or to be critical of ourselves and our preconceptions, it remains appropriate . . . that we turn to science. (Merleau-Ponty 2004: 42)

And in his lectures on nature, he describes science as 'experience in its most regulated form' (Merleau-Ponty 2003: 87). Human beings must pursue knowledge, rationally and systematically acquired, if they are to have a complete view of the world; and 'science', as has also been said earlier, is just our word for that kind of knowledge. Classical modern science required us to see the world, including ourselves and other human beings, as 'an object spread out in front of us' (Merleau-Ponty 2003: 85), something which we looked at from a position outside it. Some of the more recent developments in science, as has also been said in earlier chapters, have suggested the importance of the position of the scientist as *within* the world which he or she studies, but this suggestion is seldom recognized in the general view of scientific knowledge as purely 'objective'.

Phenomenology, as Merleau-Ponty conceives it, is not in the business of questioning the validity of science as such, or of the general view of the world with which science has to operate; but it is concerned to question some essentially *philosophical* conceptions of the world and ourselves which are based on extending the scope of the scientific world-view beyond the limits within which it has some meaning. In the radio talks referred to just now, Merleau-Ponty goes on to say:

> The question which modern philosophy asks in relation to science is not intended either to contest its right to exist or to close off any particular avenue to its inquiries. Rather, the question is whether science does, or ever could, present us with a picture of the world which is complete, self-sufficient and somehow closed in upon itself, such that there could no longer be any meaningful questions outside this picture. (Merleau-Ponty 2004: 43)

This need to see the limitations of a purely scientific, and so purely 'objective' picture of the world is particularly pressing when we come to consider our own part, as human beings, in this picture.

Can we look on ourselves purely 'from the outside', as a particular kind of object in the world? Merleau-Ponty's answer is a firm 'No'. To attempt to do so immediately runs up against the problem that this 'objective view' is necessarily a *view*, and views are held by *people*, on the basis of their own experience. Science itself is the product of experience, and so a complete picture of the world cannot leave out experiencing subjects. I cannot, as Merleau-Ponty says, regard myself as 'a mere object of biological, psychological or sociological investigation' (2002: ix), because investigation requires investigators. Even if I myself am not doing the investigation, I am involved because it is my subjective experience which makes the concepts used by the investigators meaningful to me. In that sense, I am 'the absolute source' of the world of science, not in the sense that I brought it into being in some God-like way, but in the sense that the scientific picture of the world can and must derive whatever meaning it has from me and others like me. If so, then my existence as an experiencing subject cannot be included in that picture. It is as if a painter were to try to paint a picture of himself painting that self-same picture – not of the reflection in a mirror of himself acting in that way, but of the action itself.

One irony about this is that the objectivist scientific picture of the world has, as was said in earlier chapters, its philosophical foundations in Descartes's arguments. In his search for absolute certainty, Descartes, as we saw, retreated further and further from the uncertainties of external existence until he finally found freedom from doubt in his sense of his own existence as a thinking subject. So Descartes too finds the absolute source of our reliable knowledge of the world in our own subjectivity. The trouble with this is that Descartes, through his method of doubt, appeared to have severed all connections between the thinking subject and the external objects that he thought about. If so, however, how could we be said to think *about* these external objects? The only solution seemed to be to treat the thinking subject as itself one of these external objects, whose relation to other objects (which we call 'experience') could be treated in exactly the same way as those between any other two objects: my seeing my desk, for instance, could be treated and analysed in exactly the same way as the relation between my camera and my desk when I am taking a photograph of it.

Merleau-Ponty's reference to the self as the absolute source shows that, up to a point, he agrees with Descartes. But only up to a point. For him, unlike Descartes, the relation between the subject and its objects must be 'bilateral': that is, the subject is what it is only because of its relation to its objects, and objects are what they are only as objects *for* some subject. Descartes's use of the method of doubt results in a contrast between the certainty of the subject and the doubtfulness of the world of objects: it is a retreat into the sanctuary of an 'inner world' from the uncertainty of the 'external world'. The thoughts which the subject seems to have 'about the world' are really not that at all, but thoughts about our inner *ideas* of the world. In this way, there is no reciprocity between subject and object: the subject has thoughts about objects, but objects have no impact on the subject. If he is to avoid objectivism, therefore, Merleau-Ponty has to show how his conviction that the traffic between subject and objects runs in both directions can be justified.

The root of Descartes's problems lies in the method of doubt itself. To say that we know something implies that we believe ourselves to have good reasons or evidence for holding it to be true. It may well be that some advances in our knowledge come about as a result of questioning the evidence we previously believed ourselves to have for some of our assumptions. For example, the great step forward from the view that our own earth is the centre of the universe, and that other bodies, such as the sun and the planets go round it, came about when astronomers questioned the evidential basis for that traditional view. It had seemed obvious to human beings for millennia that the sun goes round the earth because they had relied uncritically on what their senses appeared to tell them: we can just *see* the sun rising and setting, and moving across the sky from east to west in the course of the day. Similarly with the observed movements of the planets. But this earth-centred view makes it necessary to see the observed movements of the planets as incredibly complex. This suggested to such sixteenth-century astronomers as Copernicus that it might be better to base our view of planetary motion, not so much on simple appearances, as on the most elegant mathematical theory – the one which gave the least complicated account of how the planets moved. The most elegant mathematical account was the one based on the assumption that it was the sun, not the earth, which was at the centre, and that the earth itself was just one among the planets, in the same relation to the sun as Mars, Venus, Jupiter and so on. So Copernicus rejected common sense as a source of evidence for our beliefs about planetary motion in favour of mathematical elegance.

In a case like this, then, there is a place for doubting or questioning existing sources of evidence for certain categories of beliefs. But we should notice two things. First, rejection of common-sense observation as a source of evidence for theories of planetary motion does not by any means entail rejecting it for other sorts of belief. If I want to know whether it is safe to cross the road, then, provided that it is broad daylight and I have reasonably good eyesight, there is no better evidence to rely on than that of ordinary observation. I must just look and see if there are any vehicles approaching. Secondly, even in formulating his astronomical theory, Copernicus did not go in for *universal* doubt of the Cartesian kind: he questioned one source of evidence in order to substitute for it a different source, which he thought would provide a better basis for claims to knowledge of that kind. So far from doubting whether anything at all could be known about the world, he sought a sounder foundation for knowledge of the world. The better evidence was still evidence *for* a subject, but it was not evidence *about* the contents of the subject's mind, but about the world to which those contents referred.

Merleau-Ponty makes these points by emphasizing that the subject is 'destined to the world' (2002: xii). It is only because we, as subjects, are *in* the world that we can have doubts about particular beliefs. To doubt, as just said, is to question the adequacy of the evidence we consider ourselves to have for some belief or type of beliefs. But it only makes sense to do that if we have some conception of what would *count* as adequate evidence with which we can compare our existing grounds for believing. To have such a conception means that we must be in the world, since otherwise nothing could count as adequate evidence for any belief. The world is, as Merleau-Ponty puts it (ibid.) the 'natural setting' for all my thoughts and perceptions. Furthermore, I can be aware of my own existence as a thinking subject only by being aware of a world in which I exist. To be aware of my own experiences is, by virtue of the principle of intentionality, to be aware of the *objects* of those experiences: I cannot experience myself as thinking unless I am aware of myself as thinking *about* *something*, as related to something other than myself which is the object of my thought. 'Truth', Merleau-Ponty says (ibid.), 'does not "inhabit" only "the inner man" [this is a reference to a saying of St Augustine's], or more accurately, there is no inner man, man is in the world, and only in the world does he know himself.' So here we come to one of Merleau-Ponty's central contentions: that being human is 'being-in-the-world'.

HEIDEGGER AND SARTRE

The concept of human being as being-in-the-world did not originate with Merleau-Ponty. He borrowed it from the philosophy of Martin Heidegger, as did his friend Jean-Paul Sartre. But he uses it in a way which is significantly different from either Heidegger or Sartre, so it will be useful to begin by saying something about their use of this concept, in order to make Merleau-Ponty's use clearer by contrast. Heidegger above all can be justifiably described as the 'inventor' of the concept, in the sense of the philosopher who first coined the term and developed its meaning in the way he used it in his philosophy. The chief preoccupation of Heidegger's thought was the problem of the meaning of being – what has traditionally been known in philosophy as 'ontology', from the Greek roots which mean 'study of being'. (As was said in an earlier chapter, Heidegger's English translators normally use a capital 'B' for the term 'Being' in this sense. But for our present purposes, that seems unnecessary and stylistically confusing.) The world that we experience is made up of a number of things, or 'beings' of different types. For example, the bit of the world which I am presently experiencing contains such things as my computer, my desk, various books, my reading glasses, the walls of the room: all of these, and other, beings are experienced by me, and I am also a being, though of a very special kind, as we shall see in a moment. I can classify these different types of being in terms of *what* they are: each belongs to a different class, defined by its specific properties, what the members of the class are made of, how big they are, what they are used for and who (if anyone) made them. But they all have something in common, namely, *that* they are – their being. It is the question of being as such, rather than the question of the classification of types of 'beings', which particularly concerns Heidegger. This is an important contrast with those relatively few philosophers in the analytic tradition, such as W.V.O. Quine, who have taken an interest in ontology. Quine sees the central question of ontology as 'what is there?'; for Heidegger, it is rather 'what does it mean to *be*?'

As Kant had recognized, being is not a *property* of things: in defining something, we don't include an extra property of 'being'. What it is is defined by its properties or characteristics and its relations to other things: a coin, for example, is (say) a metal disc which is used in buying and selling goods. My idea of a coin is my idea of something with these properties. A *real* coin is something more than an *idea* of one: there is a difference, as Kant puts it, between having an idea of a thaler [a coin] and having an actual thaler in one's pocket. But the difference does not consist in having an extra property of 'reality' or 'being', in addition to those of being metallic, disc-shaped, etc. The question then becomes, what does it mean to say that something which is defined by certain properties actually *is*? This question Heidegger saw as central to philosophy, though it was largely neglected in modern philosophy. It is a question about the concrete reality of the things we actually encounter in our experience, rather than about the abstract classification of concepts, which is the concern of much recent philosophy. And it is also about the understanding of ourselves and our relation to that concrete reality.

But there are different *ways* in which something can 'be': there are different forms of being. A full account of ontology, one which really makes clear the meaning of being, must take account of these different ways of being. Phenomenology, in Heidegger's view, can be seen as a *method* to be used in ontology in this sense: a method for recognizing the different ways in which something can 'be'. This is an essentially subordinate position: phenomenology is of value only as a means to the end of ontology. Increasingly, as Heidegger's thought develops, phenomenology becomes of secondary interest and ontology occupies centre stage. As we have seen in an earlier chapter,

Heidegger defined phenomenology as a method which lets that which is evident show itself – which 'uncovers' that which is really evident, but whose evidence we normally ignore, because it is hidden by the assumptions which we make. Phenomenological ontology will thus consist in letting the meaning of being reveal itself, and it will do that by considering the concrete reality of the beings we encounter in our experience.

This gives a central place in ontology to *our own* being, our being as human beings. For the being of other things is revealed in *our* experiential encounters with them, so that our mode of being must take a different form from that of other beings, and must have a special significance. In Heidegger's view, one of Husserl's greatest insights was his revival and refinement of the concept of intentionality of experience: the claim that experience must always be *of* something distinct from itself. The being of an experiencer must consist, if this is so, in the *relatedness* of that being to others. Human beings are experiencers; so to be human, or to be in the special way that humans are, is thus to be essentially related to things outside oneself, and to raise the question of being, both for those other beings and for oneself. Human being is unlike the mode of being of the things which we experience, in that it consists in the capacity to question its own and others' being. My desk cannot ask itself what 'being' means, either for itself or for me, but I can raise the question of being both for my desk and for myself.

To refer to this human mode of being, Heidegger uses the fairly ordinary German word *Dasein* (which literally means 'existence', and even more literally 'being-there'). Since most translators and commentators follow him in using that German word, we shall do the same in this text (and from now on shall use the word as if it were a native English expression, without italics). Dasein thus has ontological priority over other ways of being, in that it alone is capable of raising ontological questions. Ontology must start with reflection on the being of Dasein, if it is to be capable of grasping the being of anything else. In fact, it must be primarily an 'analytic of Dasein', an analysis of our mode of being; or, as Heidegger also says, a 'hermeneutic' of Dasein, that is, an attempt to understand the meaning of our conceptions of being. Phenomenology is 'analysis of, or hermeneutic of, Dasein'. This makes phenomenology sound like introspective psychology once more, a view which was rejected in an earlier chapter. But despite appearances, that is not what Heidegger is saying. We have to remember that Dasein's being consists in its relatedness to others, so that analysis or hermeneutic of Dasein is not a matter of reflecting on the contents of our minds, but reflecting on our relationship to other beings. We understand the structure of reality by understanding ourselves; but we also understand ourselves by understanding the structure of reality.

This is indeed one of the ways in which Heidegger began to diverge from Husserl – although in his later, posthumously published, work Husserl seems to have been converging once again with Heidegger. There was a tendency in Husserl's earlier conceptions of phenomenology to talk as if he saw it as an investigation, not of the empirical contents of the human mind (what he dismissed as 'psychologism'), but at least as an examination of certain a priori structures of mind as such, which could be studied even if the world outside the mind did not exist. Heidegger's view, by contrast, is that we as experiencers cannot, because of intentionality, separate our minds from their engagement with reality, so that reflection on our own being goes hand in hand with reflection on our relationship to being as such. This is why the human mode of being is described by Heidegger as 'being-in-the-world'. To be human is to be-in-the-world.

Of course, in a sense *all* being is 'in-the-world': the only way to exist is to be part of a world. But Heidegger reserves the term for the special way in which humans are 'in-the-world': we are not like objects, who simply respond passively to other objects, which are just what they are and where they are by chance, and which are defined as what they are, not by themselves, but by us. We are in the world in the sense that we can *question* our own being and that of others, can reflect on the being of things and ourselves, and so can define ourselves. But although our being is special in this way, its special nature does not consist in being *apart from* the world, but in the particular way in which we *relate* to the rest of the world. Above all, we define ourselves in terms of our relation to other beings: our being is not transcendental, but consists in our engagement with other beings. As the term 'engagement' implies, this is primarily a *practical* rather than a *theoretical* relationship. The things around us get their meaning from the part which they play in our projects, not from some purely intellectual categorization: or rather, any theoretical relation we may have to other beings is possible only once we have already found them to be part of our world in a practical and emotional sense. Theorizing about things is based on a kind of abstraction of certain features of those things from the total reality which is what we actually experience. For instance, I experience an orange as a fruit which is juicy and good to eat; but I can abstract its shape (roughly spherical) from its other properties and then consider the sphere as a figure in geometry. But until I have experienced things like this, which have the property of being spherical as well as other properties, I can give no meaning to the concept of a sphere.

Heidegger's concept of our human mode of being as being-in-the-world is thus a way of emphasizing what is concrete over what is abstract; of starting one's philosophizing from where one is, rather than, as in traditional metaphysics, and even in some of Husserl's attempts to characterize phenomenological method, starting from a point outside the real world – the 'view from nowhere' which has been referred to so many times above. As such, it is, as Merleau-Ponty says, part of the movement of modern thought away from abstract metaphysical systems which attempt to incorporate everything into a single logically coherent whole and towards a more 'existential' kind of philosophy, concerned with truth as we experience it in our lives – as we 'live' it – rather than with a more metaphysical concept of truth as something to be gained by abstract reasoning. Starting from where we are, we cannot grasp the totality of things in one vision. We can arrive only at a provisional truth, as it is seen from our perspective. Nevertheless, this perspective is on the world: if we can be free as far as possible of preconceptions derived from past philosophy, we can gain insight into what the world is essentially like.

Jean-Paul Sartre, as said earlier, also took up Heidegger's notion of 'being-in-the-world'. In his major philosophical work, *Being and Nothingness*, which is sub-titled 'An Essay on Phenomenological Ontology', he, like Heidegger, seeks to use a phenomenological method to arrive at an analysis of being, and in particular of the human mode of being. In the Introduction to the work, he distinguishes two types of being, being 'in-itself', which is the kind that 'phenomena' or the things we experience have, and being 'for-itself', which is the kind that our consciousness of these things has. But in Part One, Chapter 1, he begins by saying that this distinction is strictly speaking a false abstraction, which talks of things which are not capable of existing in isolation as if they could be considered separately. 'The concrete', he goes on to say, 'can be only the synthetic totality of which consciousness, like the phenomenon, constitutes only moments. The concrete is man within the world in that specific union of man with the world which Heidegger, for example, calls "being-in-the-world"' (Sartre 1969: 3).

The separation of consciousness from phenomena sounds plausible, Sartre argues, if we start, as we must do in a critical philosophy, from a questioning attitude towards the world. To question is, as it were, to step back from the things which are being questioned and so to create a kind of gap between the questioner and what is questioned, which Sartre calls 'negating' the phenomenal world which is being subjected to questioning. The questioning consciousness thus, he says, introduces a 'nothingness' into the heart of being: to raise questions about something is to open up the possibility of giving negative answers – to say what something is is necessarily also to say what it is *not*. Nothingness is thus, he concludes, a necessary part of the being of which we form part, and it comes into being because of that aspect of ourselves which raises questions – our consciousness of things. Consciousness, being-for-itself, is thus really a kind of *non*-being, a nothingness: it is the negative part of being, while nonconscious things are wholly positive.

This is a curious line of thought. It starts from the claim that consciousness and phenomena cannot be separated, except by a false abstraction: the being of consciousness, concretely expressed, is being-in-the-world. But then, by making the functioning of consciousness primarily a matter of subjecting phenomena to questioning, Sartre arrives at the conclusion that the being-of-consciousness is really non-being. In one sense, this non-being cannot exist in isolation from the being of phenomena, since the questions exist only as questions *about phenomena*. Non-being and being might be conceived like the 'yin' and 'yang' of Chinese philosophy, conventionally represented as a dark and a light segment of the same circle. But all the same, to describe consciousness as non-being and phenomena as being does seem to introduce a real distinction between the two: non-being can surely not be described as being-in-the-world. Sartre seems from this point on to have abandoned the existential, or concrete, view of human consciousness as being-in-the-world, and reverted to a more traditional Cartesian view of the conscious subject as having a distinct sort of existence from material things (what Sartre calls 'the in-itself'). The rest of his philosophy thus becomes more Cartesian than truly 'existentialist', even though Sartre is usually thought of as the archetypal existentialist.

The root of the trouble lies in Sartre's concept of questioning. It has already been said that Descartes's method of universal doubt wrongly assumes that it is possible to doubt all of our beliefs all at once, and that this is what leads him to his conception of the thinking self as capable of existing in isolation from the 'external world' of matter. This is a wrong assumption, because, as already argued, we can doubt one belief only if we do not doubt others: doubting, one might say, is not total withdrawal from the world, only, as Merleau-Ponty would say, a slackening of the threads which bind us to the world. In doubting, we are '*semi*-detached', rather than completely detached.

In the same way, we could reject the connection which Sartre makes between questioning and negation. To see this, we could make use of one of Sartre's own most striking examples. I have arranged to meet my friend Pierre at the café at 4 o'clock this afternoon. I go along at 4 o'clock and find that he is not there. I look round the café for him. I see various things which definitely *are* there, and which are in that sense part of the reality of the café, but I don't find him. His absence is, Sartre would say (and in a way rightly), as much a part of the reality of the café, for me at least, as the presence of the objects I can see there. His absence is a kind of negative fact about the place. And this negativity enters in because of my disappointed expectation of seeing him there: so in that way, the 'nothingness' is created by my consciousness – it is an aspect of the café *as it appears to me*.

This is an interesting and thought-provoking example, but we can ask whether it really leads to the conclusions that Sartre wants to draw from it. I expect to see Pierre in the café, and this expectation is disappointed. Because of this, I find the absence of Pierre as much a part of my awareness of the café as, say, the presence of the glasses on the tables – indeed, in some ways, a more important part. Absence is, of course, in one sense a negative feature. But it does not follow that recognizing the absence of someone or something from some scene is 'negating' it, in the sense of separating oneself from it. Just as one can only doubt one thing if one does not doubt many others, so one can recognize the absence of something only by contrast with the presence of many other things. I am aware of the café as a whole – my consciousness of it is, because of the principle of intentionality, essentially connected with all the objects in it. One way in which I relate (positively) to the café is that I expect to find Pierre there. It is only because of that that I can feel my disappointment at the fact that Pierre is *not* there. In other words, we have to be in the world, to be connected with objects in the world, in order to have the capacity to recognize such 'negative' features of situations as absences.

Sartre thus first (correctly) recognizes that an existential, or concrete, view of our place in the world requires that we see our own being, not as that of a 'for-itself' or consciousness which is distinct in nature from the 'in-itself' of objects, but as the 'union of man with the world' which Heidegger had called 'being-in-the-world'. But he then almost immediately reintroduces the separation of the 'for-itself' from the 'in-itself'. The result is that he sees the self as entirely empty, as something to be invented by our absolutely free choices of action, not only undetermined but even unaffected by what we have been in the past, or by our present physical or other situation. (It is true, to be fair to him, that he does at times stress the importance of the 'situation' in which we find ourselves for the exercise of genuine freedom, but this emphasis unfortunately runs counter to the main thrust of what he has to say in the rest of *Being and Nothingness*.) This is not a genuinely 'existentialist' view of human beings, but a reversion, as said above, to a Cartesian view of the essential human being as disembodied and so outside the material world, timeless and placeless and unaffected by the chances of time and place.

BACK TO MERLEAU-PONTY

For Heidegger, the idea of being-in-the-world is a way of rooting phenomenology in the concrete existence of human beings in the world – as opposed to the original Husserlian conception of it as a method which involved standing back from involvement with the world. Merleau-Ponty, however, rejects this interpretation of the relation between Heidegger's and Husserl's phenomenology. Phenomenological reduction, he says, 'belongs to existential philosophy' and 'Heidegger's "being-in-the-world" appears only against the background of the phenomenological reduction' (Merleau-Ponty 2002: xvi). Historically, it has to be said that this reverses the real order of things. Husserl did, in those of his writings which were published after his death, revise the notion of the phenomenological reduction, making it more 'existential'. Phenomenological reflection, in this later version, did require a consciousness of its dependence on our unreflective involvement with life, and for that reason, as Merleau-Ponty says, could never take the form of a complete detachment from the world in which we exist. But this development, some commentators would say, came about because Husserl felt the need to meet the points made by Heidegger. That is, the revised conception of the phenomenological reduction 'appears against the background' of Heidegger's 'being-in-the-world', rather than the other way around.

In most respects, Merleau-Ponty's conception of being-in-the-world follows Heidegger's original, but there are also important differences between the two conceptions, with consequences for our view of what philosophy is and what we are like as human beings. Firstly, as implied in the previous paragraph, Merleau-Ponty wanted to fit the notion of being-in-the-world into a general framework of a developed phenomenology: his major works published in his lifetime involved a conception of philosophy as phenomenology in this developed sense. Heidegger, by contrast, in the works which followed his masterpiece of 'phenomenological ontology', *Being and Time*, moved more and more in the direction of seeing philosophy as *ontology*, setting aside to a large extent the qualification 'phenomenological'. (In his tantalizingly incomplete work *The Visible and the Invisible*, which was published only after his death, Merleau-Ponty too became more 'Heideggerian' in this sense, and expressed dissatisfaction with the phenomenological emphasis of his earlier writings; but this 'ontological turn' does not feature in most of his works.) By setting the idea of being-in-the-world in the context of the later version of the phenomenological reduction, Merleau-Ponty came to see the philosopher as a 'perpetual beginner' who 'takes for granted nothing that men . . . believe they know' (2002: xv). But he also saw the 'reduction' as limited in scope: we could not face the world altogether without presuppositions, since our reflections were rooted, as said above, in our unreflective involvement with that world.

The other major difference from Heidegger is Merleau-Ponty's strong insistence on the close connection between *embodiment* and being-in-the-world, which is not at all emphasized by Heidegger. For Merleau-Ponty, unlike Heidegger, to 'be-in-the-world' is inseparable from being a living organism. Merleau-Ponty's view of what it is to be human is in a certain sense a *biological* one, though we shall need to make clearer just what that sense is. He certainly does not want to identify our being with that of our bodies as particular kinds of physico-chemical objects, indeed he explicitly rejects that identification (see Merleau-Ponty 2002: xiv). The body as a particular kind of object is what is studied by the science of biology: it is the body considered without reference to *whose* body it is. A biological scientist can study her own body as much as anyone else's as an example of this kind of object, in a purely detached manner. So to say that Merleau-Ponty's view is biological is not to say that he regards human beings simply as objects of this kind of biological science. The 'objective body' of biological science has a location in objective space and time, but my thoughts do not (ibid.).

But besides this objective body, there is also what Merleau-Ponty calls the 'phenomenal body' (see Merleau-Ponty 2002: 121ff.). This is our own body as experienced by us, 'from the inside', 'a body which rises towards the world' (Merleau-Ponty 2002: 87). It is the body considered as particularly *our* body: in other words, where it matters whose body we are talking about. I cannot regard my own body in this sense in a detached and purely 'objective' or 'third person' way, as I might do if I were interested in it only as just one example of a human body. It is *my* body, the one through which my thoughts and feelings, as it were, 'make contact' with objects, so that there is a world for me: it is the body as the 'first person' subject of experience. But this is still a *biological* conception, in that my thoughts and feelings can exist only in the contacts they make with objects, and so can exist only in connection with a living body. The phenomenal body is what I experience 'in the manner, for example, in which my hand moves round the object it touches, anticipating the stimuli and itself tracing out the form which I am about to perceive' (ibid.). I do not make contact with the world through simply thinking about it, but through experiencing it with my senses, acting on it, in ways ranging from the most sophisticated technology to the most primitive unreflective movements, and having feelings about it, which again range in their complexity and subtlety.

It is this contact with the world through my own body which results in objects having meaning for me: the things around me are experienced, not as detached objects, but as having practical, emotional, sensual and imaginative meaning. Because human beings are, for instance, sexual creatures – beings whose bodies are equipped with sexual organs and with the corresponding bodily urges – we normally experience the world and other people as having a sexual meaning for us. Our thoughts and desires may not have a location in *objective* time and space, but they do have a place within the 'phenomenological' world, the world not of objects detached from ourselves and each other, but of meanings related to our (ultimately bodily) ways of responding to and acting upon it.

Being-in-the-world in this peculiarly human way is thus being in it as both an object and a subject, and such that the objective and the subjective aspects of our being mutually condition each other. Human beings are in the world as objects, in that they are a kind of living organism, a kind of animal. As such, they are affected, just like other objects, and in particular just like other living things, by the influences playing on them from the outside. As lumps of matter, they have mass and occupy a certain volume of space, and some aspects of their movements can thus be fully explained by the ordinary laws of physics and chemistry, such as Newton's law of gravitation or the chemical laws governing internal bodily processes. But as *biological* objects, they also act upon their surrounding environments, as when human beings act purposively, to achieve some goal of their own – even something as simple as picking up a piece of food to eat it. These purposive actions, of course, involve physical movements, and so the action is only possible if the laws of physics and the laws derived from them do not rule out the possibility of the relevant movement. To take a simple example, someone whose arms are paralysed cannot exercise her intention to pick up a piece of food in order to eat it. But, to the extent that the action is purposive, we need, as we have seen in the last chapter, to explain it also in terms of its purpose. Why did she move her arm in that way? Because she wanted to pick up some food in order to eat it.

Equally, our being as subjects has to be understood in terms of our being biological organisms. That means that our subjectivity is not that of some 'inner self', which merely contemplates the world. Rather, what we are as human beings is not purely 'inner', but is, as Merleau-Ponty puts it, 'through and through compounded of relationships with the world' (2002: xiv). We exist as subjects only through our relationships to objects outside us (including, as we shall see in Chapter 7, other subjects). And because we are biological organisms, not all those relationships with objects, as we have seen, are high-flown or intellectual. Even those which are intellectual, such as our theoretical reflections about things, can be understood only against the background of our pre-reflective involvement with the world. We have to be in the world before we can begin to reflect about it, and above all before we can begin to reflect about our being-in-the-world. Where Descartes went wrong, in Merleau-Ponty's opinion, was in separating thought from the world that we think about: if it is indubitable that I exist as a thinking being, then it is equally indubitable that the world I think about exists.

The world is meaningful for me because I am engaged with it, primarily in unreflective ways, but then secondarily in reflective ways. For that reason, the meanings which objects in the world have for me are not *given to* them by me, or by my thoughts about them, but are *discovered in* the objects themselves. There is no room, therefore, for philosophical idealism in Merleau-Ponty's thinking – that is, for the doctrine that reduces the reality of things to that of the ideas that we have of them. One of the best-known idealist philosophers, the eighteenth-century Irish thinker Bishop Berkeley, summed up this view in his doctrine that 'to exist is to be perceived', or in other words, that things can exist only to the extent that they are thought about by someone. To say that our being is 'in-the-world', however, is to imply that the world exists independently of our thinking about it. The world has to be there in order for us to think about it; and our very experience of it is as something 'inexhaustible', to use Merleau-Ponty's word: there is always something more of it to be experienced, beyond what we have experienced so far. 'The world', Merleau-Ponty says, 'is an open and indefinite unity in which I have my place' (2002: 354). I am just a *part* of the world, not its creator, and it is impossible to have a subject without a world for that subject to be conscious of. My experience of the world is always from a certain perspective within it, and is limited to what I can perceive from that perspective.

Nevertheless, there is a sense in which Merleau-Ponty would admit that Berkeley got it right. My place in the world is, indeed, among infinitely many possible places, but at the same time it is more than just one among many. This may seem to be self-contradictory, but that apparent inconsistency should hopefully dissolve when we investigate further what Merleau-Ponty has to say. The sense in which Berkeley has got it right, he says, is that we cannot conceive of any object which is not perceivable by us (see Merleau-Ponty 2002: 373). 'The world' for us means 'the world as we experience it, or are capable of experiencing it': in that sense, the world is simply the correlative of our experience. And certainly, the unity of the world as a meaningful structure is necessarily the correlative of our experience of it as such: the world without experiencing subjects could not be said to have any meaning at all, since a meaning is always *for* someone. The world as meaningful is not a world 'in-itself', a world as it would be if no one experienced it (the world as viewed from nowhere). But it is the 'setting of our lives', the pre-existing stage on which we act out our lives, including our thoughts.

This is confusing and difficult to make sense of, but does that mean it is unintelligible? One way in which Merleau-Ponty tries to help us to make sense of it is by means of the model of a dialogue. 'The whole of nature', he says, 'is . . . our interlocutor in a sort of dialogue' (Merleau-Ponty 2002: 373). If we are engaged in a discussion with someone, that person is clearly *other than* ourselves; we can talk to ourselves, but then we conceive of ourselves metaphorically as two people, and think as if one 'half' of ourselves is conversing with the other 'half'. The whole idea of a conversation involves at least two different people. At the same time, the other person in our dialogue is not completely 'other': as a partner in the dialogue, she is necessarily linked to us. What she says is a response to what we say, and *vice versa*. The meaning which we find in her responses is not *imposed* by us on her words, but discovered when we try to decipher what she is saying. At the same time, her words have to be meaningful *to* someone else (such as ourselves) if they are to be meaningful at all. In that sense, words become meaningful only in the interaction between speakers, in a 'dialogue'.

Being-in-the-world is, for Merleau-Ponty, like engaging in a dialogue with objects. In living our lives, we necessarily engage with the world in various ways, practical, emotional and theoretical. We can do this only because the world is already there to be engaged with, just as we can have a dialogue only if there is another person there to talk to. In taking part in such a dialogue, we 'transcend' ourselves, we open up our thoughts to a wider reality which is independent of us. But at the same time, there is a sense in which the existence of the dialogue, and the meaning given to the 'responses' to our involvement depends on us. We give unity to the world by our dealings with it; but also we gain unity in our own selves, and even in our own bodies, from our dealings with the world. It is by scanning an object with my eyes, or manipulating an object with my hands, that my different experiences of the object are unified into the experience which constitutes a single self. In this way, the world can be both an absolute Other, there already before we experience it, and also indissolubly related to our experience of it. Our being-in-the-world makes a difference, both to the character of the world and to our own existence.

In this way, Merleau-Ponty manages to combine elements of both objectivism and subjectivism, both realism and idealism. There is an objective or real world, independent of our experience, which our experience must reach out to if it is to be an experience at all. Even to speak of our experience as 'perspectival', as such that it must be from somewhere or other, implies that it is a point of view *on* a world on which other points of view are also possible. This is the source of the appeal of objectivism: even to talk of ourselves as experiencing the world from our own point of view requires us to be able to arrive at a wider, more universal, point of view by 'comparing notes' with other subjects. As said before, this more universal point of view will be 'objective', not in the sense of a 'view from nowhere', which is impossible, but in that of a 'view from everywhere'. But it is something to which we are bound to aspire as soon as we begin to experience the world. Although this explains the legitimate appeal of objectivism, however, it also makes clear what is mistaken about the misleading interpretation of objectivity which has prevailed in our culture since the Scientific Revolution of the sixteenth and seventeenth centuries. It is a fatally easy move from saying that we need to think of a world which is common to all experiences, and is in this sense independent of any single experience, to the conclusion that there is a world 'in-itself', independent of experience as such. The truth in subjectivism or idealism is that the concept of an experience without a subject, and without a perspective, is meaningless.

We can close by going back to Sartre. Sartre, as we saw, while in theory accepting the idea of human existence as 'being-in-the-world', in practice for most of his writings reverted to a Cartesian view of human beings as unsituated subjects or 'nothingnesses'. If we are unsituated, then we have no distinctive individual characteristics, since our individual characteristics are defined by our relations to other things and people, that is, by our situation. What differentiates me from other individuals has to do with my gender, my age, my upbringing and the characteristics derived from it, and so on. Sartre at times acknowledges this, but it is inconsistent with the main thrust of his thinking. His concern is mainly with affirming human freedom, which means rejecting the idea that elements in our external situation might *determine* our actions. But the conclusion which he draws is that such characteristics do not even *define* us, or give us our identity. If they do not, however, then there is no 'us' to act anyway. As Sartre himself quite rightly says, freedom must be 'in a situation': I can make choices only if there are real alternatives facing me between which I have to choose. But then these alternatives must not themselves be chosen, otherwise we should end up with the absurdity of an infinite regress: I can choose only because I am in a situation defined by x, y and z. But if this definition of my situation is itself chosen, then there must be a second-order situation which determines the parameter of *that* choice. And, if the second-order situation is then defined only by my choices, then there must be a third-order situation, and so on and so on *ad infinitum*. In his drive to maximize human freedom, Sartre ends up making our situation also the result of choice, and so loses the advantage gained by accepting that choice always implies a situation. We need to see human freedom in more concrete terms, as an ordinary making of choices in a world we did not choose. This is more genuinely 'existentialist' than Sartre's view, because it places human beings squarely in concrete situations which set limits to their freedom. Merleau-Ponty, with his account of being-in-the-world, is in this way much more genuinely 'existentialist' than Sartre.

CHAPTER 6

TIME

SPACE AND TIME IN NATURE

The objectivist view of space and time, as one might expect, is that they are objective, in the sense of existing in complete independence, not only of individual experience, but of human experience altogether. This is essentially the account of space and time which is presupposed by classical Newtonian physics, and is often called the *Absolute* conception. It is the idea of space and time as a kind of permanent framework, existing independently of any particular perspective, in terms of which objects and events can be located in a completely determinate fashion. My computer, for example, is *here*, and where 'here' is in this case can be defined completely in terms of its position relative to other objects, which themselves can be located with equal determinateness, ultimately by reference to the universal framework of Absolute Space. Similarly, my writing these words is taking place *now*, and when the relevant 'now' is can be determined completely by reference to the framework of Absolute Time.

Merleau-Ponty, as said earlier, was by no means hostile to science, and would not for a moment wish to deny the utility of the idea of an objective framework of space and time, on which not only science but our everyday use of calendars and clocks depend. (Though, for many scientific purposes, as he would also say, the classical Newtonian ideas of Absolute Space and Time have been set aside since Einstein.) What he would want to question as a phenomenologist, however, is the leap from the utility of these ideas to metaphysical assumptions about the meaning of the 'objectivity' we are talking about here. It is central to his version of phenomenology that no term at all can have any meaning for us unless it is rooted in our direct, pre-reflective, contact with the world in experience. This must apply equally to the terms 'space' and 'time'. Our concrete experience of space is centred on ourselves: 'here' is where I am, and other objects of my experience are located by their relation to 'here'. Some things are nearby, others further away: the window of my study is currently to the left of me, while the door is to my right; the ceiling is above, the floor below; and so on. In much the same way, 'now' is defined by what I am presently experiencing. My writing these words is part of what counts as 'present' for me, whereas my writing of the preceding page is part of my past, and my visit to friends this evening is in the future. Past and future are defined by their relation to the present, and the present in turn is defined in relation to my experience. What I call 'now' is, of course, related to what other experiencers also call 'now', but there is no way in which 'now' can be defined without reference to *some* human experience.

All this is, of course, so obvious that it might seem to be not worth saying. But phenomenology is in large part a matter of reminding ourselves of what is obvious to us when we are not theorizing, in the face of our constant tendency to give our theoretical conceptions a higher status – to treat them as in some way more fundamentally *real*. We can perhaps see this better if we consider an example, one which has been used before in this book. In our everyday thinking, we talk of the sun as 'rising' and 'setting', of its 'disappearing below the horizon' after sunset and 'coming over the horizon' at dawn. All this talk implies that it is the sun which moves and the earth on which we stand which remains still. Since Copernicus, however, the scientific view has been that it is the earth which moves, and that the sun's motion is merely apparent, the result of the changes in our perception of it due to the motion of the earth. Which view is correct? The answer is surely that *both* are, depending on the context in which they are asserted. For the purposes of astronomy, it is true to say that the earth is a planet which, like other planets, moves relative to the sun. This is the view which gives us the simplest and most elegant account of planetary motion, and that is what we require for scientific purposes. But it does not follow from that that we are wrong to say, in a more everyday context, that the sun rises and sets, that it is directly overhead at noon, and the like. Sunrise, noon and sunset are important points in our organization of the day. In societies without artificial lighting, people rise at dawn and go to bed after sunset; but even in our highly technological society, although we may get out of bed much later than dawn and go to bed long after sunset, the 'movements' of the sun give a pattern to our days.

Moreover, the astronomical conceptions of planetary motion round the sun only have any meaning for us as a kind of abstraction from ordinary experience. The movement of the earth round the sun is what we would see if we could view the solar system, not from earth, but from a position outside the system. This point of view is the one we need to adopt for scientific purposes, but it is not a 'view from nowhere', just a view from a different perspective. It is certainly a *wider* perspective, not limited by our position on the earth; and so it is in principle available to any being whatsoever who is capable of developing scientific astronomy, wherever in the universe they may be located. But a wider perspective is still a perspective; and this particular one is available only to beings who are capable of developing a perspective from where they happen to be, beings who are capable of a *subjective experience* of the world. We have developed the Copernican view by abstracting from our everyday perspectives, and imagining ourselves as seeing the earth from the outside, as one other body moving through space. Just by virtue of being *perspectives*, all these views are 'subjective', in the simple sense that a perspective must be such *for someone*. But none of them is 'subjective' in the derogatory sense that it is an *illusion*: there is a difference between fantasies about the sun's motion and our everyday perception of it as rising and setting. We have a subjective perspective only because we are *in* the world – we are a kind of object, in the sense of being living organisms. Thus, space, for embodied subjects, cannot be a simple invention or projection of our minds: it is the medium in which we exist.

We can say similar things about time, which has a more important place in Merleau-Ponty's thinking than space. The objectivist notion of time has no room for ideas of time 'flowing' from the past through the present to the future: these terms, as said earlier, are after all defined in relation to each other and ultimately to human experience. The only notion of time which can be admitted to an objectivist picture is one based on relations of 'before' and 'after', which are thought to be definable without reference to human experience. The year 2000 comes before the year 2001 and after the year 1999 – notice how the tense of the verb in this sentence is *present*, as if all the years were displayed together in a single 'eternal present'. Merleau-Ponty uses the example of a river, which, in our ordinary ways of speaking, we say flows from the melted glacier in the mountains down through the plain to the sea. But if we consider the river 'in itself', that is, without any relation to human experience of it, then, Merleau-Ponty argues, we cannot think of a succession of events in this way (the melting of the glacier producing the water which flows across the plain and ultimately joins the sea). Indeed, we cannot even speak from this point of view of 'events' at all: 'the very notion of event has no place in the objective world' (Merleau-Ponty 2002: 477). An 'event' is something which has a beginning and an end, which are defined by their relation to other events happening in the past and in the future, so that to define something as an 'event' requires us to use the notion of 'the past' and 'the future', which are not 'objective' terms. All we can say about the world 'in itself' is that the melting of the glacier comes before the flowing of the river across the plain, which in turn comes before the joining of the river and the sea.

But can we even say this if we are thinking in strictly objectivist terms? To say that A comes before B and B in turn before C surely is to say that A, B and C form a *succession* of events, that they have some kind of special relation to each other, such that B 'flows out of' A and C out of B? Even within themselves, A, B and C are surely successions of events. The melting of the glacier, for example, consists of different stages related to each other – the heating of the ice followed by its slow transformation into water. And this succession can only be divided from the next, the flowing of the water just produced down the hillside, by someone who *thinks of* them as distinct events. When we talk of the melting of the glacier as followed by the flowing of the river-water, we are, Merleau-Ponty argues, implicitly thinking in terms of an observer who has successive views of the different stages of the river. If we did not think of time from the point of view of someone who is *in* time, then we could not, he says, think of time at all (see Merleau-Ponty 2002: 482). Even the time of nature thus requires a basis in subjective time, or, as Merleau-Ponty puts it, 'historical' time.

But this must not be misunderstood. Once again, we see Merleau-Ponty giving a new sense to the terms 'subjective' and 'objective' and to the relation between them. To say that time is fundamentally subjective might be taken, by someone still immersed in objectivist assumptions, to mean that it is 'unreal', purely imaginary, a human invention. But that is not what Merleau-Ponty means. The time of past, present and future is subjective in the sense that it can exist only if there are subjects who are capable of experiencing it in that way (see Merleau-Ponty 2002: 526). But it does not follow that it is unreal or invented by those subjects. The subject for Merleau-Ponty, it must be remembered, is essentially embodied, and the body which, in that sense, we are is itself a part of nature. Bodily processes 'unfold' in natural time: the very real fact of their succession is what 'projects around the present a double horizon of past and future' (Merleau-Ponty 2002: 278). And it is our shared experience as embodied human beings which creates the idea of a single unified time, the same for everyone: the only meaningful sense of 'objective' in relation to time is 'generalized' (see Merleau-Ponty 2002: 526).

In relation to both space and time, then, Merleau-Ponty sees the source of misunderstanding as the objectivist tendency to separate too sharply 'subjective' and 'objective', 'in itself' and 'for itself'. If we, as phenomenologists, strive to free ourselves from such objectivist assumptions, then we can recognize both that natural time is rooted in subjective or 'historical' time, and that natural time is the basis of historical time. Human beings in a sense 'create' both time and space, in that a world without conscious subjects such as ourselves would be one in which 'time' and 'space' would have no meaning. But equally, because our subjectivity is embodied and our being is in-the-world, time and space provide the objective framework in which our existence unfolds. There is no contradiction here, as long as one properly understands what is meant by 'subjective' and 'objective'.

HUMAN TIME

As for Heidegger, being-in-the-world is essentially temporal: as body-subjects, our existence is necessarily in time, a time which is always being constituted and which is therefore never fully constituted (Merleau-Ponty 2002: 482). It is even misleading to say that our existence is *in* time: what we should rather say is that it *is* time. We are aware of ourselves as subjects in so far as we are aware of ourselves as having intentions to act in one way or another – 'projects' to fulfil. I, for instance, currently have the project of writing this book, and also that of going for a walk when I have finished work on it for today. Having an intention of this kind is, Merleau-Ponty says, a way of 'transcending oneself', a way of going beyond what one has been in the past and projecting one's existence into the future, when (hopefully) one's intention will be fulfilled. The part of my book which I am writing today 'grows out of' the parts which I have written on previous days. Future parts will in turn grow out of today's work, and the whole will eventually, if all goes well, constitute a complete book on Merleau-Ponty. Time – past, present and future – is in this way the very medium of existence as a subject. As an active being who forms intentions, I carry with me in my present a sense of what has been, of the past, as well as feeling the future weighing down upon my present. The past, the present and the future 'do not all three have their being in the same sense' (Merleau-Ponty 2002: 482); if they did, the past would not be different from the present and the future, so that time would not exist at all. In this way, existence as a subject necessarily has a *direction* and a *meaning* (the French word *sens* can be translated by either of these two words in English). At the beginning of his chapter on 'Temporality' in *Phenomenology of Perception*, Merleau-Ponty quotes from the French poet Paul Claudel, who said, 'Time is the *sens* of life'. Claudel is here playing on the double meaning of *sens*, as is shown by the way he goes on: '*sens*: as one says "the *sens* (direction) of a water-course, [or] the *sens* (meaning) of a phrase"' (Merleau-Ponty 2002: 476).

Temporality is at the heart of being-in-the-world. Being-in-the-world is not, as we have seen, standing outside the world looking on, as a timeless subject such as God might be supposed to do. It is being actively involved with the world, acting on one's situation to change it, but only in ways which the unchosen character of the situation will allow. One's situation in the present is what it is because of what it has become, that is, because of the past (including one's own past); one's actions to change it will be completed in the future; and the succession of past, present and future is what gives unity and direction to one's life. The actions which one performs confer meaning on one's situation, and the direction of one's life as a whole could be described as its meaning. In this way, temporality is the link between ourselves as subjects and the world of objects that we perceive. It is not *in* objects in themselves: things in themselves, independently of consciousness, could not be said to 'develop' or 'unfold', since such terms have meaning only for a conscious being who can be aware of the world as consisting of things which both have a continuous existence over time and also change from one state to another. But equally, consciousness does not have the power to constitute time: it is caught up in a time which moves forward independently of it. Temporality is in this way an aspect of what Merleau-Ponty calls the 'ambiguity' of our existence in the world – the way in which our existence is both part of the world and capable of standing back from it, or at least of 'loosening the ties which bind us to the world'.

This ambiguity provides the background for Merleau-Ponty's account of human freedom. Like Sartre, he affirms that we can be free *only* in a situation; but unlike Sartre, he consistently follows through the logical implications of that affirmation and develops a conception of freedom which is not absolute. An important part of anyone's 'situation', which imposes constraints on her freedom, is her own past, including her own past choices. Given that we are embodied subjects, our past choices are 'sedimented' in our body, in the same kind of way that past geological changes now form part of the fabric of the earth as we experience it today. For instance, someone who is a confirmed gambler will have formed certain habits of response and behaviour, which continue to influence his present actions because they are expressed in continuing bodily patterns: in, for example, patterns of brain activity involved in behaving in these ways. This sedimentation does not make change impossible, but it does make it difficult: the gambler is free to give up his gambling, but he cannot do so by simply resolving to give up. He needs to reinforce that resolve by finding ways of breaking the gambling habit.

In this way, freedom can be understood only in terms of the temporality of our existence. Our present constantly transcends our past, in the sense of going beyond it, but the nature of the transcendence is itself shaped by what has gone before. The past does not *determine* our present actions, but it does provide the *context* in which we choose to act. Each time the gambler acts, whether to indulge in further gambling or to make a resolve to overcome his gambling habit, he is making a choice which goes beyond what he has been in the past. This is most obvious in the case where he decides to try to give up gambling. But it is true also of the case where he carries on as before: to 'carry on as before' is to extend the past sequence of actions into the present, to be someone who not merely *has been* a gambler, but someone who *still is* one. This is essentially bound up with the temporality of our existence: the past no longer exists, but is nevertheless a necessary horizon for our present experience – the present is thus bound up with the past, but also necessarily goes beyond it. And the present itself is a transitional phase between the past and the future, so that the future also provides an open horizon for the present. Real freedom is not, and cannot be, separation from our past, starting life entirely anew. Rather, it is taking up the challenges posed to us by our past and seeking to find answers to them which will shape our future. Like a river, which is carried forward by its own internal force, but only along channels which the surrounding environment makes possible; so our lives proceed in their own direction, but only in ways which are made possible by the inner constraints of our own past and by the outer limitations of our present situation. (There will be more discussion of Merleau-Ponty's views on freedom in the next chapter.)

BECOMING ME

This discussion of freedom and temporality naturally leads on to thinking about personal identity – about the question of what makes a person the individual he or she is, distinct from other individuals. What is it that makes me me, and you you? In the history of modern philosophy since Descartes, there have been many views of the nature of personal identity. For Descartes himself, what I am is identified with my *mind*, conceived of as a 'mental substance', something which has only mental properties (essentially consciousness) and is capable of existing independently of any other substance, especially material substance or body. To be me as opposed to you is then to be *this* mental substance which is responsible for my thoughts, desires, wishes, feelings and so on, rather than *that* one – the one which is responsible for your different thoughts, etc. And to go on being me over time is to have the same 'mental substance'. Descartes's near contemporary, the English philosopher John Locke, rejected the idea of 'mental substance', since according to him the concept of 'substance' was an obscure one: no one could know therefore whether our thoughts, feelings, wishes, etc. inhered in a substance at all or in a substance distinct from our bodies. Still, Locke held that our identity as persons depended on our mental attributes, or, in a word, in our consciousness of being who we are, whatever kind of substance, if any, that consciousness inhered in. My being me, for Locke, consisted in my *consciousness* of being me.

One serious difficulty in both Descartes's and Locke's accounts of personal identity is that I, presumably, do not cease to exist or to be me when I am unconscious, having no thoughts or feelings at all – as in a dreamless sleep or a coma. A connected difficulty is that we may well suspect that thoughts, feelings, etc. depend for their existence on something *non-mental*, on our brain: this suggests that it is our brain which is more fundamental to our identity than the thoughts which arise when our brains are active, and this would also explain how I can go on being me even when I am not mentally active or even conscious. In this way, we could arrive at what might be called the 'materialist' theory of personal identity: to be me is to be a particular human being, a particular physical organism. This organism, being human, can of course engage in thought, but need not; and it is the organism with which I am to be identified, not any of its activities.

Despite the obvious differences between the accounts of Descartes, Locke and the materialists, there is one important feature that they have in common. None of them seriously take account of temporality. In one sense, they have to take account of time: after all, the identity of something which exists over a period of time, as a person does, is not only identity at a time, but also identity *through* time. Locke is explicit about this: his account of personal identity is primarily meant to be an account of what it means to be the *same* person, the same 'me', at different times. And the other theories we have considered can give answers to that question. The problem lies with the answers that they give. Something, like a person, that endures through time will change in many ways. A person grows older, learns new things, behaves in different ways at different stages in her life, remembers some things and forgets others, and so on. If we are to speak of these as changes in the same person, we shall need to provide some link of continuity which connects them up in some appropriate way, to preserve identity through change. For Descartes, the link must be that the changes are in the accidental properties of an unchanging mental substance: the mind remains the same, but it has different thoughts, desires, motives, etc. at different times. But this cannot be right. If the whole being of a 'mind' consists in having thoughts, how can the mind remain unchanged if its thoughts are always changing? Is not the adult in some important sense no longer the same *person* as the child? The idea of a mental substance *sounds* as if it is doing some work in providing connective tissue, as it were, to link together the changing thoughts. But when we examine the idea more closely, we see that it does not do any such work at all. Furthermore, it cannot account for the fact that our thoughts, etc. do not merely *change*, but *develop*: that is, that our thoughts as adults are what they are in part because of what our thoughts were when we were children. Our personality develops in the way that the plot of a novel or other narrative does – the later phases do not merely succeed the earlier, but grow out of them.

Locke, as we have seen, rejects the idea of an underlying mental substance. For him, therefore, consciousness must be presumed to maintain its continuity by itself, without support from any substance. Something called 'consciousness' must remain unchanged, while what the person is conscious of changes: as a child, the person has one kind of thought, as an adult a different kind, but what links the two is that the adult is conscious of, or remembers, the childish thoughts as part of her own past. But this is even more obviously open to the criticisms which were made of Descartes: there is literally *nothing* over and above consciousness to do any connecting work, and consciousness can, as said, not be separated from its changing contents. We might express the point by asking what it is which makes a present memory of a child's experiences into *my* memory of *my* childhood, rather than just a thought about *someone's* past thought? There seems to be nothing in Locke's theory to make the difference, so that there is even less connection between the changing thoughts to make them all into thoughts of the same person. And what was said about Descartes's failure to explain the *development* of the self applies even more clearly to Locke.

The materialist's problems appear at first sight to be slightly different. Materialists do, after all, provide something concrete to link together changing thoughts, namely, the brain. The different thoughts I have at different stages in my life are, on this view, linked by being all thoughts occurring through the activity of the same brain. But this does not really solve the problem; it only shifts it. For the brain itself is constantly changing, as is the rest of the human body. The brain loses cells, the rest of the body both loses old cells and gains new ones. Patterns of connection within the brain are changing all the time as the person is faced with new experiences. Even if one accepts the materialist's account of the relation between 'mind' and 'brain', therefore, we cannot distinguish between changing thoughts and an unchanging brain or body. And the materialist is just as much faced with the problem of the development of the person as Descartes and Locke. Increasing complexity of the brain over time does not seem to offer any better explanation of the way in which adult thoughts differ from, but grow out of, those of childhood. Adult thoughts are distinguished from childish ones not merely because they require greater brain-power to think them (as Einstein's thinking about space and time might differ from mine): they differ in being more 'adult', more sophisticated, based on a wider experience of the world and people.

Faced with these sorts of problems, some philosophers, such as David Hume in the eighteenth century and Derek Parfit in the twentieth, have understandably tried to rethink the whole question of personal identity. Perhaps, they suggest, when we talk about 'personal identity', we are not really talking about *identity* in the strict sense at all. Maybe there does not need to be any connecting link between the different stages of what we choose to call the 'same person's' life; talking about 'the same' person is perhaps just a convenient way of referring to certain sequences of thoughts and other experiences which we find it socially useful to pick out from others. What we call a single self is, according to Hume, just a way of talking about a 'bundle of perceptions', a collection of experiences which happen to be related causally, but in no deeper sense. It is like the way the different buildings on the same site and all called 'St Mark's Church' are referred to as 'the same church' only because we have some reasons to regard them as such – they all serve the same parish, the later versions have retained, not only the name, but many of the records of the previous versions, and so on. And Parfit argues that so-called personal 'identity' is not really strict identity at all; we decide, he says, to treat some sequences of experiences as those of 'the same person' only because we see the 'psychological continuity' between the various sequences as being particularly strong. Parfit compares this with the way we talk of a group of people existing over time as 'the same nation'. This is not because there are real connections between the groups at different times (the composition of the group, for example, obviously changes over the centuries, and they may even occupy different territories). It is because we (or they) decide there is sufficient 'historical continuity' between the group of that name at one time and the group of the same name at a later time. This is called a 'reductionist' approach to personal identity, because it explains away the appearance of genuine identity by reference to something else which gives rise to that appearance.

But this approach faces difficulties of its own. If it is true that we have *reasons* for grouping together different phases of a person's (or a nation's) life and so making them into parts of a continuing narrative of the same person's/nation's existence, then surely there *is* a real connection between the different stages – it is not some kind of arbitrary invention on our part. Compare this with a different case. If I find a number of books in a room and decide to arrange them on a shelf to make the room look a bit tidier – say by putting together all the books of the same size – then there is no real connection between the books on the shelf: their linking together is a mere invention of mine. But if I put together all my texts of and commentaries on Merleau-Ponty on the same shelves, and call it 'my Merleau-Ponty library', then the 'library' has a real unity, because there is a genuine linking thread connecting the different books with each other. In the case of a person, this is even more obviously the case, since the different stages of the same person's life are connected, not merely by happening after each other, but by developing out of each other.

Descartes, Locke, the materialists and the reductionists all fail to do justice to the temporality of human identity in that they, in their different ways, treat the different stages of a person's life as being in time only in the sense of occurring one after the other, in much the same way that a random sequence of notes played on the same piano occur one after the other. They are linked accidentally in that all the notes happen to be played on the same piano, but they have no other connection with each other: it could equally well be that each note was played on a different piano, and then there would be no connection between them – they would constitute a genuinely random sequence. This is *natural* time, the time of before and after. But the temporality of human personal existence is not like that. It is more like that of a symphony, in which the notes are connected up and given a unity in that they are part of the development of a theme, or of interrelated themes. The symphony exists in *historical* time, just as the life of a person does. It has a past, a present and a future. The note or notes which are being played at present (let us say as part of the second movement) do not merely occur after those belonging to the first movement, but have an intelligible connection with them: we can fully understand what they are only by understanding how they are related to those of the earlier movement. And they do not only occur before those of the third movement: they have to be understood as *anticipating* the later notes.

A person's life, according to Merleau-Ponty, is temporal in the same sense of 'historical' time. It is always open to us, of course, to analyse a person's life as if it were a natural object, and so to see it as a sequence of events in natural time. This is the objectivist stand-point, adopted for instance by a psychologist who examines the causal relations between a person's childhood experiences and his or her adult behaviour. The coldness of a father's attitude to a child, for example, may be said to cause certain kinds of behaviour in that person when he becomes an adult, such as a desperate search for a 'father-figure' who will respond to him more warmly. But this objec-tivizing attitude to a person can exist only because we already rec-ognize him as a single person, and the particular causal connection can make sense to us only because we already understand how a parent's coldness can affect our view of ourselves and so motivate us to behave in certain ways. We gain the ability to recognize the unity of a person's life, and the ability to understand the connections between stages in life, from our own case – from the experience that we have of being a single person, with a past, present and future which interrelate in various ways. Natural time gets its meaning from historical time, and the objectivizing approach is an abstraction from the direct experience which is described by phenomenology.

I am not an object in the world, but a point of view on objects. Even to say that, however, is to imply that my existence as a 'self' con-sists in my relation to objects – that is what it means, after all, to say that human being is being-in-the-world. My existence as a subject is not, as Descartes and Locke would say, an existence as something which can be accessed by me alone, nor, as materialists would say, as a particular kind of object, my body or perhaps my brain. The self which I am aware of in experience, before all such 'theories of self-hood', is what I am aware of in acting. Merleau-Ponty quotes from the French poet Valéry, who said, 'The work of the mind exists only in act' (Merleau-Ponty 2002: 36). I experience the unity of my self in that my past, including my past choices, gives me the motives and reasons for my present actions, which have their consequences for my future. The unity of myself, as it presents itself to me in pre-reflective experience, is thus not that of something unchanging which under-lies the surface changes, but of something which is perpetually changing, but in which the changes are related to each other to form a developing sequence. What I am is what I am perpetually coming to be. My life does indeed unfold in historical time, and its unity does consist, as Parfit would say, in a historical continuity. But where a reductionist like Parfit goes wrong, as Merleau-Ponty would see it, is in implying that this historical continuity is not a genuine unity, and in seeing my life history as a mere succession of events, rather than as something which is developing in an intelligible way. I can understand my present in the light of the past from which it has come – and others can understand my present in the same way.

MERLEAU-PONTY AND FREUD

This picture of the self as developing – as constantly becoming, but in a way which makes the present intelligible in the light of the past – when combined with his notion of the essential embodiment of human subjects, enables Merleau-Ponty to give a particularly illuminating interpretation of Freudian psychoanalysis. Like most French intellectuals, especially in the period from the 1920s to the 1950s, Merleau-Ponty was intrigued by Freud's theories and their apparent potential for shedding light on the vagaries of human behaviour and for alleviating mental disorder. But he was dissatisfied with the conceptual framework in terms of which Freud expressed his theory, and believed that a more phenomenological interpretation of psychoanalysis would make the value of what Freud was saying more evident. Freudian psychoanalysis is not as fashionable as it was among orthodox psychiatrists, especially in the English-speaking world, but it is possible that the kind of interpretation of it that Merleau-Ponty offers might make its claims more acceptable.

Freud himself was medically trained, and was steeped in the respect for mechanistic science which was so characteristic of thinking in the late nineteenth and early twentieth centuries. He thought of himself as a scientist, and of his theories as part of a biological account of human nature and behaviour. This is essentially, in Merleau-Ponty's terms, an objectivist view of the study of human behaviour. The language in which Freud expresses himself is an objectivist language, describing human beings as simply a particular kind of object in the world, whose behaviour could be causally explained as the outcome of physical forces. To simplify a little, Freud saw human actions as the result of certain biological 'drives', pressures which built up inside the human organism and needed release, in much the same way that a head of steam might build up in a machine and need to be 'let off' if a dangerous explosion were to be avoided. The energy behind these drives was called *libido* (the Latin word for 'lust' or 'sexual desire'), which was equated with the instincts for survival as an individual and for sexual activity, which was necessary for the survival of the species. This *libido* was present throughout one's life, including in infancy: it was held to develop through various phases, in which different parts of the body – the anus, the mouth – became in turn the focus of sexual interest until finally, if all goes well, sexuality came to be centred on the genitals. The powerful force of *libido* needed to be directed and tamed if ordered society was to be preserved. This control of *libido* was most obvious in early childhood – children's sexual activities and desires needed to be directed. Problems arose, however, when, as a result of the child's relationships with parents, the development of *libido* was 'fixated' at one of the pre-genital stages. The very memory of the original problem was 'repressed', kept out of consciousness, so that the person became unable to move beyond the stage of development at which he or she was fixated. This was the major source of mental disorders in adult human beings, because of its continued effects on the adult's behaviour. Psychoanalytic therapy consisted in talking with patients in such a way as to bring the repressed material to the surface and so enable patients to resolve their problems in full knowledge of what lay behind them.

Merleau-Ponty did not have any quarrel with Freud's empirical work, his actual accounts of cases and how he had dealt with them. But it seemed to him that the conceptual framework in which Freud formulated his theoretical description and explanation of that work was misleading. It presented a 'third-person' view of human beings and their behaviour, and attempted a causal explanation of the things people do. The therapy involved patients adopting a third-person perspective on themselves, getting to know what lay behind their own problematic thoughts and actions. But our pre-reflective (and indeed our reflective) awareness of ourselves is, Merleau-Ponty argues, from a *first-person* perspective: our desires and thoughts are not things we contemplate, but things we *live*, ways in which we 'are-in-the-world'. And there are other difficulties springing from Freud's objectivist assumptions. First, his account of repression makes it sound as if the mind is a *place*, a kind of container for thoughts, desires, wishes, etc. Thoughts and other mental contents, when repressed, are, as it were, pushed down into the lower chamber of this container, which Freud called 'the unconscious', where they are kept out of sight. But apart from the phenomenological difficulty that our actual pre-reflective experience of our own minds is not of them as *things* or objects in this way, there is also the problem of how something which is kept out of sight in this way can still be said to influence the 'visible' part of our behaviour. Secondly, thoughts, desires, etc. are thought of by Freud as internal, mental things, accessible in principle to introspection, rather than as ways in which we relate to objects outside ourselves. But again, this is not how we actually experience our own thoughts and desires: they are part of ourselves, experienced in the first person, not third-person objects to be contemplated. Finally, sexuality is thought of, in objectivist fashion, as an impersonal biological force which somehow directs human actions from the outside, rather than as something which has a first-person meaning for human beings.

If we are to do justice to the first-person nature of mental life, we need to reconceptualize Freud's account. First of all, we need to think again about Freud's concept of *libido*. In using this term, Freud was in effect seeing sexuality as all-pervasive in human existence. But what does this mean? If we identify sexuality with genital activity, then *libido* must be defined as the drive towards the specific goals of genital activity. But if so, it cannot be all-pervasive, since not all human goals are genital in nature. On the other hand, if we make *libido* all-pervasive, it comes to mean little other than a generalized 'life-force' and loses all really precise meaning and explanatory power. What we need, if we can get it, is a concept of *libido* which has some kind of specific connection with sexual activity, but is not limited to sex in any narrow sense. How can we get such a concept? Somehow or other, we must make sexuality into 'a manner of being in the physical and inter-human world', while not losing its specifically sexual content, its relation to genital activity (see Merleau-Ponty 2002: 184).

Merleau-Ponty finds the answer in his concept of the body-subject: our existence as persons is essentially embodied, while our bodies are what they are because they are the bodies of persons. Our personal existence is rooted in our biological life and needs, but 'takes up' these needs and gives them a personal form, as a way of being-in-the-world. One of our crucial biological characteristics is, of course, our sexuality. Indeed, as Merleau-Ponty says, 'the sexual apparatus has, running through it, the general current of life' (2002: 184). But because our biological or bodily life is that of a person, sexuality takes on a personal *meaning*. This does not mean, however, as Merleau-Ponty emphasizes, that it loses it character as something bodily: to say that someone's sexuality can be fully understood only if its personal meaning is grasped is not to reduce it to something purely 'spiritual' (indeed, nothing in human life can, in Merleau-Ponty's conception, be described as 'purely spiritual', without bodily content).

In order to explain his point more clearly, Merleau-Ponty considers a particular example (see Merleau-Ponty 2002: 185ff.). He speaks of a girl who has been forbidden by her mother to have anything more to do with her lover. The girl, as a consequence, comes to suffer from insomnia and loss of appetite and, worst of all, loses the power of speech. An orthodox Freudian explanation of her condition would, as Merleau-Ponty says, refer to the 'oral phase' of sexual development, during which, in Freudian theory, *libido* is focused on the mouth: the girl would presumably be said (Merleau-Ponty does not go into detail here) to 'regress' to this phase because of her sexual frustration, and so would express her frustration by symptoms involving the use of the mouth, for eating and for speaking. But matters are more complex than this, Merleau-Ponty argues. The meaning of the mouth and its uses may well have sexual relevance: no doubt, he accepts, the girl may be 'particularly sensitive' to the throat and mouth because of problems in the oral phase of her development. But these parts of the body also have a wider significance. Speaking is closely related to our communal existence, our relationships with other people: in refusing to speak, therefore, the girl is expressing her wish to break off from relations with others, in particular with her family. Eating, again, is a natural symbol for the assimilation of things from outside, which is part of the normal flow of existence. In refusing food, therefore, the girl is expressing her inability to 'swallow' her mother's instruction to her to avoid contact with the young man she loves.

Sexual development plays an important part in the story: the girl's condition, after all, results from a prohibition by her mother of a sexual relationship; and her response to this prohibition focuses on her mouth and throat, not only because of the wider significance of these parts of the body, but also because of their significance in sexual development. The total situation is at one and the same time 'personal', in the sense of being about personal relationships with other human beings (her boyfriend, her mother) and 'sexual', in that the relationships in question, or one of them at least, have a sexual dimension in a perfectly ordinary sense of the word 'sexual'. In an embodied subject, the same behaviour can have both personal and sexual significance, and the two are inseparable from each other: our personal relationships are part of the current of our existence, which runs through our sexual apparatus, and our sexual feelings in turn are bound up with our personal relationships with other human beings. Sexuality is central to human existence because sexual experience is 'an opportunity . . . of acquainting oneself with the human lot in its most general aspects of autonomy and dependence' (Merleau-Ponty 2002: 194). It is a 'dialectic', 'the tending of an existence towards another existence which denies it, and yet without which it is not sustained' (ibid.).

One thing which is worth emphasizing is the way in which Merleau-Ponty uses language which implies that the girl *actively chooses* to respond in the way she does. The emotion, he says, 'elects to find its expression in loss of speech'; the patient 'tends to break with life itself'. At the same time, Merleau-Ponty makes it clear that his use of this language is not meant to imply that the girl makes a *conscious* choice to respond in these ways: she does not, as he says, 'mime with her body a drama played out "in her consciousness"' (2002: 186–87). This too follows from Merleau-Ponty's view of human beings: neither as merely disembodied minds, nor as simply biological organisms, but as body-subjects. Our responses can be personal even without being conscious, and expressed through our bodies without being merely passive effects of causal stimuli acting upon us. The girl's problem was a *human* one, not merely a biological or merely a 'psychological' one. It was resolved, as Merleau-Ponty says, by psychotherapy, which took it seriously as a human problem, and by the withdrawal of her family's prohibition on her seeing her boyfriend. When that happened, she regained her speech and her desire to eat.

This also indicates how Merleau-Ponty interprets the other key Freudian concept, that of 'repression'. For Freud, the memory of certain traumatic events in childhood was 'repressed', in the sense of being 'pushed down' into a region of the mind where they could no longer be readily called into consciousness. The result, as said earlier, was that the person was supposed to 'regress' to an earlier stage in development and to lose the knowledge of what was going on inside her which would have given her the capacity to alter her own behaviour by conscious choice. But Freud's objectivist assumptions about human beings tempted him into treating repression, not as something which a person *does*, but something which *happens to* the person as a result of external influences. This is what Merleau-Ponty wants to question, in the light of his phenomenological account of human beings as embodied subjects who have their being-in-the-world. Being embodied in the way that human beings are is not a matter of being an object acted upon by external forces. It is rather a matter of having certain 'projects', certain *active* ways of dealing with the world around oneself. Repression, in this light, comes about when someone enters upon one of these projects, finds an obstacle to making progress with the project, but does not have the capacity to overcome the obstacle. The result is that the person continues to make the attempt, and remains at the stage at which the problem first arose. This fixation at a particular stage is 'sedimented' in the person's body, in the form of habits of behaviour and response which belong to the stage at which he or she is fixated. At the level of explicit thought, things change: 'but this process of renewal touches only the content of our experience and not its structure' (Merleau-Ponty 2002: 96). On the surface, the person looks and behaves like an adult, but the adult behaviour is itself influenced by the surviving habits of an earlier phase in life. This is where, according to Merleau-Ponty, neurosis arrives. Repression is not the pushing down of memories into a part of the mind called 'the unconscious': the mind is not an object, and so has no parts. Rather, it is the sedimentation in bodily habits of responses to problems which no longer really exist – a sedimentation which interferes with the person's capacity to respond to adult, problems in adult ways. Equally, the treatment of neurosis does not consist, as it is often represented, in getting the patient to recognize the existence of the material which has been repressed. Rather, it consists in forming a personal relationship between the doctor and the patient, so changing the patient's mode of being-in-the-world in a way which makes it possible for the patient to accept the meaning of his or her disorder – that is, which reintegrates the repressed feelings into his or her life.

Merleau-Ponty's reinterpretation of Freud thus brings together his notions of the body-subject, of being-in-the-world, and of the temporality of human existence, shown in the way in which the person does not have a static identity, but one which develops through time. In the next chapter, we shall see how these same ideas can shed light on the way in which human beings live together with each other in society.

CHAPTER 7

OTHER PEOPLE, SOCIETY, HISTORY

THE PROBLEM OF THE OTHER

None of us lives an entirely solitary existence: even the hermit's desire to separate himself or herself from the presence of others depends on a recognition of the reality of other people – they are indeed all-too real for the hermit, absent but not non-existent. But some philosophical theories imply the possibility that others might genuinely not exist, or might exist only as ideas in one's own mind. To illustrate this, we can go back again to Descartes's account of our existence as essentially *inner*: we exist as minds, which can be accessed only by ourselves, and we could so exist even if it were not the case that there was anything other than our own minds. His division between 'mind' and 'body' depends on the premise that minds *could* exist on their own, and perhaps will actually do so in the after-life. So, if Descartes is right, we can at least conceive the possibility that there are no other people than ourselves. Of course, we have the *idea* of other people, but such ideas may just be the result of our own imaginings. And there seems to be no way in which we could prove otherwise, since the only evidence we can have for anything consists in the ideas we have in our minds. (Descartes argues that, on the basis of the ideas we have in our minds, we can prove the existence of a God who is benignly disposed to us and so would not deceive us about anything so fundamental. But his arguments for the existence of God are logically flawed, and anyway it seems a desperate move to invoke God in order to prove anything as self-evident as the existence of others.) For all I can know, therefore, I may be alone in the universe, and all my apparent dealings with other human beings may be just the product of a fond illusion.

This seems to be a pretty absurd conclusion to draw, and that suggests that the premises from which it is drawn may be faulty. The main culprit is clearly Descartes's view of the self as purely inner, an object in some kind of internal and non-physical 'space'. The materialist philosophers who rejected that view of the self, and saw human beings simply as a particular kind of material object in the world, obviously avoided thereby the particular form of the problem of the 'Other' with which Descartes was faced. But they ran into other kinds of problems. For if they are right, then I am just one of these human objects, and others are beings of the same type. The only relations between me and them must therefore be of the 'objective' kind which can exist between any two objects. If my fist comes into contact with another human being's face with a certain force, it will cause injury to that face, just as if a hammer came into contact with it with the same force. But it is clear that, to the extent that we think of other human beings as other *people*, we have all kinds of relations with them which cannot be assimilated to those between two objects. These relationships depend on mutual recognition of each other as *subjects*, as beings capable of thoughts, feelings, wishes, desires and so on. For instance, if I work with someone, that is not a matter simply of our two bodies moving in more or less the same ways, but of our mutual recognition of each other as fellow-workers with shared goals, which we try to achieve by cooperating with each other. A materialist might not have Cartesian problems about the existence of other human beings, but would have difficulties in distinguishing other people from other kinds of object.

Merleau-Ponty, as we have seen already, rejected both these views of the self. To be human, for him, is certainly to be more than a 'mind': even minds can exist only as engaged with objects, just as objects can form a 'world' only to the extent that we engage with them as such. Human being is not purely 'mental': we are embodied subjects, and the mode of existence we have is being-in-the-world. But we are embodied *subjects*, not just material bodies. We *experience* the world, each from his or her own point of view; we are not simply passively affected by it. Even an object can be an object only *for* some subject or, rather, subjects. But we also necessarily experience, as part of our world, other subjects – other people, like ourselves, who share in the same world. If, like true phenomenologists, we try to describe the world as we actually experience it, rather than, like objectivists, redescribing it in the way we assume it *must* be, then we shall accept that, as soon as we experience the world, we are conscious, not only of objects, but of other subjects. Indeed, even to speak of experiencing a 'world' which is 'inexhaustible' and not created by me, is to imply that it is one on which other perspectives than my own – those of other subjects – are possible.

The world in which I find myself when I begin to have any experience at all is, of course, one of 'nature' – of non-human objects arranged in natural space and time. But it is also a *cultural* or human world. I find around me, not only hills, trees, lakes and the like, but also streets with buildings in them, fields which have been fenced off, tools, tables and chairs, knives and forks, television sets and other artefacts (see Merleau-Ponty 2002: 405). These things are just as real as the physical objects I experience: I can see them, touch them, manipulate them in just the same way. And they cannot be reduced to their purely physical characteristics. The knife and fork I use to eat my meals might be described by a physical scientist as pieces of metal of a certain mass, a certain shape and certain dimensions, but that is not the only correct description of them: it is just as correct to describe them as a 'knife' and a 'fork'. Nor is the scientist's description somehow more fundamental. Rather, the reverse is the case. Knives and forks are not made only of metal, but of a variety of materials, and they do not all have exactly the same shape or size. What makes them 'knives' and 'forks' is the *use* to which they are put, and the materials and physical properties are relevant only to the extent that some materials and properties would make them useless. A knife made of paper, for instance, would not be of any use for cutting up meat, or even for cutting through butter.

Being defined in terms of their human use or relevance indicates something else important about such objects. Their use is a use *by someone*; their relevance is a relevance *for someone*. Their very existence as humanly relevant and humanly used entities depends on some human being or other. In being aware of cultural objects like this, then, I am aware of other human beings. These human beings are, as Merleau-Ponty puts it, 'anonymous': I can recognize a knife and fork as things to be used by someone for eating meals without knowing *who* precisely that 'someone' is, and as made by someone, without knowing the name of the maker. What they embody is what Hegel and other philosophers have called 'Objective Mind': they are the results of human thought, but not necessarily that of any particular named individual. And once they were created, they became 'objects', with a life of their own independent of that of their maker or makers. If I make a table knife, or write a book, then as soon as it is completed what happens to it will be determined by factors other than my wishes. My knife may be left out in the rain and go rusty, or melted down by someone else to make a metal toy; my book will be either read by others or left to gather dust in the bookshop or library. Even if I retain ownership of my own products, I cannot guarantee that these things will not happen to them.

Being-in-the-world is thus being-in-the-*social*-world, as well as being-in-the-*natural* or physical-world. Human beings live in a culture, not just in nature. Indeed, the concept of 'nature' is itself a cultural concept. Nature, Merleau-Ponty says, 'does in fact follow the experience of cultural objects, or rather it is one of them' (2002: 28). 'Nature' primarily means what human beings recognize as such: what provides the background to human life and human culture. As human artefacts are made of natural materials, human structures are supported by their foundations in nature, and human beings themselves live and have their thoughts because they can derive air to breathe and food and water to eat and drink from nature. The objectivist concept of nature as consisting of a collection of objects and their qualities, existing in complete independence of human experience and without meaning or value, actually *falsifies* what we mean by 'nature'. Even the 'nature' of science is, in a sense, a human construction, in that it involves seeing the world outside us as classified in various ways and ordered by laws of nature, making it something intelligible and predictable to human beings. Merleau-Ponty does not object to the scientific concept of nature as a tool for science, but only to the philosophical assumption that its role in science makes it a more accurate conception than any other. To repeat what has been said in an earlier chapter, this is not philosophical 'idealism'. It is not the absurd claim that what stimulates our experience is somehow created by that experience, but rather the perfectly reasonable claim that what we mean by 'nature' must be those stimuli as conceptualized by human ways of thinking.

The world that we experience is, in that sense, a *human* world as well as a *natural* world – indeed the human world is in some ways prior to the natural. We find ourselves in a world along with other human beings, who share with us the meanings which objects around us have. Language plays a vital role in this awareness of a shared world. We discover the meanings of things in the concepts we share with others, which are embodied in the language we speak. What I see from my window is a 'street': it falls under the concept of a 'street' which exists in our culture and is embodied in the language spoken in that culture (in this case, English). A child has to *learn* this language; until she does, what is going on around her will be only vaguely and indeterminately meaningful. To use Merleau-Ponty's analogy, the child will be like the spectator with a poor seat at the theatre, who sees the responses of the other members of the audience, their laughter, their tears, their shouts, but cannot really grasp what it is that is provoking those responses (or therefore what exactly those responses are – are the members of the audience really *smiling*, or *grimacing*, or *opening their mouths wide*, or what?). We learn our language, not primarily by attaching words as 'representations' to what they represent, but by learning to *do* things: we learn the meaning of a word, Merleau-Ponty says, as we learn to use a tool, 'by seeing it used in the context of a certain situation' (2002: 469). We can see strong similarities between Merleau-Ponty's account of language and meaning and that of the later Wittgenstein. And, again like Wittgenstein, Merleau-Ponty sees the learning of language as part, not only of dealing with the world, but also of our relations with other people (see Merleau-Ponty 2002: 470).

Being-in-the-social-world, then, is not, as the materialists might say, being a physical object among others, with whom we have purely physical relations – spatial, temporal and causal. It is being aware of the world as shared with other human beings who are subjects like ourselves, beings with whom we share the meanings given to natural and cultural objects, and with whom we can therefore communicate. This is also the basis of Merleau-Ponty's answer to those philosophers such as Descartes, whose views of the mind as purely 'inner' make it possible that there may be no other conscious beings in the universe except ourselves. The usual name in the history of philosophy for this kind of position is 'solipsism'. Solipsism (which comes from the Latin words *solus ipse*, meaning 'oneself alone') is the doctrine that I am, or at least might be, the only conscious being in existence. If so, then the apparent existence of other beings, and especially of other conscious beings, would be just an illusion, like that of the real existence of the creatures which figure in our dreams. That solipsism in this sense is untenable is implied by Merleau-Ponty's claim that we cannot give any meaning to the term 'world' unless we can share that term with other subjects: I could not speak of 'my world' (or therefore of 'myself') unless I could also speak of 'other people's perspectives on the world', and so of other selves. There is a sense, however, in which Merleau-Ponty can and does accept a kind of solipsism. The very fact of there being different selves entails that my thoughts, emotions, sensations, wishes, desires, and so on are distinct from yours, or hers, or his. If this were not so, then no problem of solipsism could arise, for the simple reason that there would be only one self, shared between all beings capable of thought and other mental activity. But that is clearly not how things are: not only are my thoughts, feelings, etc. distinct from yours, but I logically cannot have yours. I cannot literally feel your pain, although we may both feel pain at the same time and caused by the same object. I cannot have your anger, though we may both feel angry with the same intensity and about the same thing. I *see* your anger as expressed in your behaviour – in your flushed face, the grim set of your jaw, your tight lips, and so on; but I do not *feel* your anger as I feel my own. And there is always the possibility that I might be mistaken in thinking you were really angry – you might be just play-acting, for example. I could usually tell whether it was real anger by making further inquiries, but I do not need to make such inquiries in my own case, and those I make in your case might leave me ultimately uncertain about the truth, especially in the case of more subtle thoughts, feelings and desires. The minds of others are indeed impenetrable, just by virtue of the fact of their being *other*. But this does not justify the kind of metaphysical solipsism discussed earlier. For unless I knew that you were a conscious being other than myself, the very possibility of uncertainty about what you were thinking or feeling could not arise.

THE SOCIAL WORLD

My 'self' is thus not the name for something radically private, accessible to me alone. I alone can *directly experience* my thoughts, feelings, wishes, desires, etc., but they are accessible in other ways to others – they see them in my actions, gestures and facial expressions, even in my 'body-language'. These actions and gestures, it is true, need interpretation, and the interpretation may be mistaken; but it is equally true that I can be mistaken about what I myself actually feel. The true nature of the experiences I have may well have to be discovered by reflection, especially in the case of more complex thoughts and emotions. Merleau-Ponty gives the example of discovering that I am in love: I may have, and probably have, already been aware of the feelings and actions which later reveal my love to me – the feeling of impatience to meet the person I love, the unusual concern with my appearance when I am going to meet her – but it is only on reflection that I come to recognize them, perhaps with a shock of discovery, as signs of being in love (see Merleau-Ponty 2002: 442). The discovery is not that of certain facts about a particular kind of object, called 'my self', achieved by 'introspection', or looking inside: it is a matter of formulating the meaning of some of the things I do, as a being in whom 'mind' and 'body' are inseparable – of my manner of being-in-the-world. It would be better to say that it is the result of 'retrospection', of reflecting on my past – another sign of the temporality of human existence.

In the same way, I can be mistaken about my own feelings – something which on Descartes's view ought to be completely impossible. I may, for instance, mistakenly imagine that I am in love with someone. This is not a mistake about my inner life. It is not comparable to a mistake which I might make about the actual properties of some object, as when I see a tomato in some peculiar lighting conditions and therefore think, wrongly, that it is black. If I discover that what I thought was true love was instead an illusion of love, this is not like realizing that my inner state did not have some property that I thought it had: I did have feelings for the person concerned, feelings which at least have some resemblance to those of someone who is genuinely in love. I said to her that I loved her, and felt a kind of commitment to her. But when I reflect on my relationship with her, I realize perhaps that these feelings and behaviour were not about *her*, but the result of her resemblance to someone else. Or I may come to understand that my sense of commitment to her was of the kind that one has to a friend, with whom one shares certain beliefs or interests, not of the kind that one has to a lover. Or perhaps I was in love with certain of her *qualities* – her smile, or her looks – rather than with the whole person who has those qualities (see Merleau-Ponty 2002: 440). Once again, the mistake is revealed, not by introspection into the properties of some inner object, but by retrospective understanding of the meaning of my feelings and actions. It is a mistake about 'the place of feeling in my total being-in-the-world' (Merleau-Ponty 2002: 441). Shedding illusions about oneself is not like abandoning a hypothesis about some object when the evidence shows it to be false. It is abandoning a certain conception of the nature of one's being-in-the-world.

Being myself is in this way not a matter of having a certain kind of 'inner life', totally separate from the inner lives of others. What I am is what I understand myself to be, in terms of 'outward' behaviour as well as 'inner' thoughts, feelings and desires. And what I understand myself to be is dependent on the concepts of modes of being-in-the-world which I share with others. As in the examples given just now, the difference between 'true' and 'false' love can be stated only by taking into consideration concepts of what love involves – roughly, a certain kind of feeling about a specific individual, considered as a whole, combined with a certain kind of commitment to him or her. This conception is the one which prevails in our culture, and is expressed in our language: where 'our language' does not mean simply 'the English language', but any language which embodies a culture which is in this respect at least like our own. The fact, for instance, that we can translate Merleau-Ponty's remarks about love from French to English indicates that to some extent at least French culture conceives of '*amour*' in much the same way that English-speaking culture conceives of 'love' (which is not to deny that, in other respects, the two conceptions are *not* the same in meaning!). It also follows that we can understand other people's feelings and behaviour in the same ways as we understand our own, by retrospective reflection on the ways in which they respond and act. And we can discuss our understanding of their, or our own, feelings with them. In this sense, to be what one is – to have the feelings, attitudes and other personal characteristics one has – is to be a member of a particular culture: to be with others in a particular way.

At the same time, of course, to be what one is is necessarily to *distinguish* oneself from others. If individuals cannot exist apart from society, then it is equally true that society cannot exist apart from the individuals that make it up. A society is a collection of individuals. But it is not equivalent to any *particular* set of individuals, in the way that, for instance, 'this sack of potatoes' is equivalent to the *particular* set of potatoes which happen to be in this sack at the moment. Societies, for one thing, endure longer than the lives of individuals: when I was born, I became a member of a society which had already existed for some time – the same society to which my parents, grandparents and so on also belonged. And when I die, the society will not be changed by that fact. Again, societies can continue to exist even when they absorb new members and lose old ones – by, for instance, immigration and emigration. In ways like these, societies have a life of their own which is at least to some extent independent of the lives of the individuals who make them up at any given time. This can be seen clearly in the case of what might be called 'sub-societies', like football clubs. The Liverpool FC whose supporters rioted at the Heysel Stadium in 1985 is the same as the one which won the European Champions' League in 2005, but of course the individual members of the Liverpool team, of the management of the club and of its supporters on those two occasions were significantly different.

Like that of individuals, the life of a society or culture changes over time. And the way in which it changes, again like individual lives, is *historical*. Just because a society is made up of individual human beings and their shared ways of being-in-the-world, the changes in its life, like those in the lives of its members, are not a succession of changes in accidental properties against the background of an unchanging 'essence'. A society is also an 'embodied subject': it is embodied in the particular, and changing, human individuals who make it up and the products of their thought, and its subjectivity is that of those individuals. Its continuity in both respects results from the fact that those individuals continue to *think of* it as the same, and express their thoughts in the 'Objective Mind' referred to earlier – in constructing cities and other settlements, institutions, values, languages and other cultural entities, and in reflecting on and having discussions about its identity. So we can say that a society or culture *is* Objective Mind. And, like individual body-subjects, it exists, not in the natural time of before and after, linked by external causal relationships, but in historical time, in which the past becomes the present which then in turn opens on to the future. Like individual thoughts, emotions and actions, the life of a society or culture can be understood as an intelligible development: the present can be understood by seeing what it makes of the past in projecting itself toward the future.

Except, of course, that 'the present' does nothing: it is an abstraction. It is *people* living in the present who make something of what they see as their past, and have a certain vision of how they want things to go in the future. 'The past', equally, is not an external force, determining what the present must be like or how we must act in the present. Rather, it is we human beings who find in our conception of the past, and in our conception of our present situation, a reason for acting in one way rather than another. Merleau-Ponty gives examples of how this works, both in the lives of individuals and societies. Suppose, for instance, I had a 'mystical crisis' at the age of fifteen: perhaps I had an overwhelming sense of a deeper spiritual reality underlying the ordinary material world, and an accompanying feeling that I should devote my life to this spiritual reality. Later in my life, I reflect on this incident from my past. I can regard it in various ways: it might be seen as just a part of adolescence, perhaps an expression of hormonal upheavals, or on the other hand as a sign of a religious vocation. Neither of these readings *forces* itself upon me: I must choose, in the light of how I see myself now, which reading to accept. But whichever I choose will have a bearing on how I act now. If I see it as merely an adolescent phase, I shall regard it as irrelevant to my life now; on the other hand, if I see it as an early sign of a religious vocation, I shall probably take it more seriously, and perhaps take it as a reason for training for the priesthood or going into a monastery (see Merleau-Ponty 2002: 440f.).

Much the same could be said about the history of a society. Merleau-Ponty refers to the decision of Napoleon Bonaparte to make himself Emperor of the French in 1799, thereby transforming the Republic which had been the outcome of the Revolution into an Empire (see Merleau-Ponty 2002: 522f.). This was a momentous decision for the future of France, but it has to be understood in the light of Bonaparte's (and other people's) reading of the immediate past: the Revolution seemed to have run its course – there was no room for taking it any further but, on the other hand, it seemed impossible to revert to the monarchy of the period before 1789. Bonaparte's solution to this problem was to establish his own military power as a new kind of system of government, different both from the traditional monarchy and from the revolutionary Republic. To us, looking back and seeing this decision as realized, this development might seem inevitable, but there is nothing predetermined about it. It arose, not from impersonal forces of history compelling people to act in certain ways, but from people's own reflections on their present situation and its relation to the past. Just as with an individual, a society is what it is by virtue of its history, or rather by virtue of what its members make of its history. The identity of a society or a culture is constituted by what it has been, and by the conception of that past that those who live in it hold: in this way, its present identity is intelligibly connected to its past. And the future of any society or culture will be what its members decide it will be, in the light of their understanding of what it has been.

Since the individual is necessarily a member of a society, clearly the situation in which an individual finds himself or herself is in part a social one. To be an individual living in Britain, say, is to be in a different situation from being an individual living in Argentina: the possible choices which are open to someone will differ, both because of the physical constraints of their situation, but also, and equally importantly, because of the constraints imposed by their society. To take one of Merleau-Ponty's own examples (see Merleau-Ponty 2002: 519), a middle-class intellectual cannot choose to become a fully fledged member of the working class. At most, he can choose to go and work in a factory and live only on the wage he receives there. But then he will become, not so much a member of the working class, in the way that someone born into that class is, as an ex-middle-class person who is now identifying himself with the workers. To identify oneself with the working class is to have a different kind of social identity from that obtained by being born and bred into that stratum of society. And it is that social identity, as perceived by the members of society, which creates the 'situation' in which individuals have to make their choices. Furthermore, since a society is, as said above, constituted by its history, the social situation which constrains an individual and affects his or her identity will also be constituted by the history of that society. To be an individual in early twenty-first century Britain will thus be different from being an individual in, say, early nineteenth-century Britain. What it means, for example, to be 'middle class' or 'working class' will be different in the two historical situations.

As we saw in the last chapter, freedom for Merleau-Ponty is always freedom *in a situation*. We have just seen how the individual's situation is created partly by the social and cultural background in which he or she acts. But it is equally true, and for the same reasons, that societies have freedom only in a situation. Society's development is not *determined* by its past, but the past of a society does set limits to the ways in which it can develop in the future. Where western society can go in the future is limited by where it is now, and where it is now is a result of where it has been in the past. We live in a society which is, for instance, based on representative democracy and market economics, a society in which science and the scientific world-view exert an enormous influence on how people think, even about non-scientific questions. We cannot therefore act as if we lived in a society of hunter-gatherers who did not engage in trade and who had a pre-scientific, perhaps an animistic, view of the world. This is not to say that we could not, if we wished, revert to something like such a society; but that would be a *conscious reversion*, and so would not be like having lived in that kind of society for millennia. The resulting society would be affected by where we started from: we could not, for example, simply forget about science and resume animism, though we could choose to suppress all the existing manifestations of science – all the laboratories, the scientific journals, the teaching of science in schools and universities, and so on. In his essay 'Eighteenth Brumaire of Louis Bonaparte', Karl Marx says that human beings make their own history, but only in conditions that they did not choose, which were transmitted to them from the past. Merleau-Ponty would certainly have agreed with this (for more on Merleau-Ponty's Marxism, see the next section).

A society or culture thus provides the framework in which individuals live out their lives and find their identities. But it is also constituted by the individuals who are its members, and the decisions which they take – both the sum of individual decisions about their own lives, and their decisions about the future development of society as a whole. These decisions are free, but are made within the constraints imposed by the social structures in which individuals live, and by the historical development of the society and its structures. All of this implies a certain view about the way we try to understand society and history. It implies that the 'social sciences' (history, sociology, economics, political science, etc.) cannot proceed in the way which has become familiar in the natural sciences – that is by 'causal explanation' in terms of general laws. For example, it is misleading to say that my situation *causes* me to belong to a particular political party, though it, or rather my understanding of it, does provide me with a certain *reason* for choosing that party rather than any other.

Merleau-Ponty uses the example of a tenant farmer who is as poor and exploited as the industrial workers in a nearby town (see Merleau-Ponty 2002: 516f.). But this does not necessarily mean that he, like them, will join a radical left-wing political party. All depends on how he sees that situation. Does he see what he has in common with the factory workers? Or does he rather blame them, with their wage-demands, for forcing up his cost of living? In the first case, he will be inclined to support the same political party as they do; in the second, he may well do the reverse and swing to the right, seeing himself as having interests in common with their employers rather than with the workers. The situation decides what possibilities there are for his decision – what are the ranges of reasons he has open to him. But it does not *cause* him to make one decision rather than another. As this example shows, we can make sense of the farmer's party allegiance, not by looking for general laws: there are no true generalizations to the effect that people who are poor and exploited will belong to left-wing parties. Rather, we have to enter into this particular poor person's thinking about his situation, and see how this is connected with his choice of party. Understanding societies, their historical development and the behaviour of people within them is thus more like understanding the meaning of words in a language than like grasping the workings of a machine.

MERLEAU-PONTY AND MARXISM

Like many intellectuals in many countries in the 1930s and 1940s, Merleau-Ponty was on the left politically. Up until the time when he was a student at the ENS, and for some time afterwards, he was a practising Roman Catholic, but he interpreted Catholic social teaching as supporting left-wing policies. He eventually gave up his faith, not primarily for philosophical reasons, but in disgust at the reactionary attitudes, as he saw them, of some in the Catholic hierarchy. As an intellectual, he then needed a new basis for his politics, which he found in Marxism. But the Marxism he espoused was not the official version adopted by the French and other Communist Parties, but the more 'humanist' interpretation advocated by a number of contemporary thinkers. One of the great influences on his thought in this respect was the Hungarian philosopher and literary critic Georg Lukács. Another was a Russian émigré called Alexandre Kojève, whose lectures on Hegel he attended in the late 1930s. Kojève interpreted Hegel in a Marxist fashion, and conversely used Hegelian concepts to interpret Marx. The result was a Marxism which was strikingly different from the official Communist version which prevailed in the former Soviet Union, at that time seen as the leader of world Communism.

In order to understand better what was at issue, we had better say something first, however briefly and inadequately, about what has so far been vaguely referred to as 'the official Communist version' of

Marxism. It was based mainly on the writings of the later period in Marx's life, when he had abandoned many of the Hegelian ideas and the utopian dreams which had influenced his youthful thinking and come to think of himself as a hard-headed scientist like those of his contemporaries who were working on further developments in physics, chemistry, biology and so on. This later Marxism was seen as 'scientific socialism', which was supposed to uncover the laws of social motion in much the same way as physics formulates the laws of physical motion. As with any other science, Marxism sought to discover causal laws, in this case laws which would enable us to understand and predict the conditions in which social change of a crucial kind must occur. Armed with a knowledge of these laws, socialist revolutionaries would be able to see when and how they should mobilize the masses in order to speed up these necessary changes: in the conditions of modern capitalist society, the necessary change would be to a socialist society, in which the exploitation of some human beings by others would cease.

The forces shaping society, according to this interpretation of Marxism, were, first, the development of humanity's power over nature (technology), and corresponding changes in the ways in which human beings could satisfy their material needs (the 'means of production'). Secondly, there were the results of the division of all human societies so far into classes, defined in terms of their relationship to the means of production. In such a class-divided society, the class which had control of the means of production would inevitably be the dominant, or 'ruling', class: economic power meant also political and social power. The other classes in society could have only a subordinate role, serving the interests of the ruling class. Because the ruling class would seek to use the whole of society to further its own class-interests, the other classes would inevitably be exploited, being mere instruments used by the dominant class. But each such arrangement contained within itself the seeds of its own destruction. The subordinated classes would feel increasingly oppressed and would eventually rise in revolt against this oppression, overthrowing the old ruling class and taking power in its stead.

The situation in 'modern', i.e. western capitalist, society was seen by Marx as promising the final overthrow of the domination of one class over others in a final revolution, which would usher in a new kind of society without classes and so without domination of human beings over other human beings. This would be a 'socialist' society, or, in its most mature form, a 'communist' society. Capitalist society contained this promise for a number of reasons. First, it was based on industry, the most complete domination possible of human beings over the rest of nature. Secondly, the way in which this industrial system developed would inevitably reduce the number of classes in society. Whereas, in previous societies, there had been several classes, each with its own interests, competing for power, now increasingly there would be only two – the ruling class, those who owned and controlled industry, known as the 'bourgeoisie'; and the class of those who were ruled, those who worked in industry to produce profits for the bourgeoisie, known as the 'proletariat'.

Thirdly, the condition of the proletariat would inevitably get worse, since the members of the bourgeoisie would have to compete harder and harder within a market economy, and so would have to drive down the wages they paid their employees in order to secure their own profits. The result would be that more and more members of the bourgeoisie would go to the wall, unable to stand up to this competition, and so drop out of their class and join the proletariat. Thus the proletariat would grow in size and strength in comparison with the bourgeoisie. Its sense of solidarity would also grow, as its poverty and oppression increased and its members realized that they were all in the same boat. Fourthly, the bourgeoisie, in its drive to create the kind of rational modern society that an industrial economy needs, would strip away all the illusions and myths about power in society that had helped to keep previous systems in order – like the feudal belief that the rulers were appointed by God and had obligations to look after those who were subject to them. The ending of these illusions would make it easier for the proletariat to rise up and overthrow the bourgeoisie. Since there would then be only one class in society, society would no longer be divided into different classes. The whole of society would have collective control of the means of production, which could therefore be used to supply the needs of all rather than the interests of a small section of society. Because there were no class divisions to control, the need for a state authority would disappear, and the state would eventually 'wither away', leaving a free, self-organizing, system in which all human beings could freely take part in deciding the path to be taken by society as a whole.

This then, in very rough outline, was the official version of Marxism. The development of capitalist society and its eventual revolutionary overthrow were regarded as being as predictable as, say, an eclipse of the sun, and for much the same reasons. We can predict when the next total eclipse of the sun will be visible in the northern hemisphere because we know the laws governing the motions of the sun, moon and earth, and the date of the next total eclipse follows from those laws together with data about the present position of these bodies. In the same way, Marxists held, we could predict that capitalist society would eventually collapse in a revolutionary socialist upheaval because that collapse follows from the laws of history discovered by Marx, together with data about current developments in capitalist economic systems. In the language we have now grown familiar with, this is clearly an 'objectivist' view of society and history. It treats human beings and their societies as just one set of objects in the world, and changes in those objects as the result of the workings of appropriate general laws, which enable predictions to be made. Human beings and societies are seen as objects, in that their subjective awareness of their situation, and its influence on their behaviour are denied, or at least disregarded: how they behave is supposed to be determined entirely from the outside, by the play of external forces on them.

In view of what has been said earlier about his conception of phenomenology as subverting such objectivist assumptions, one would not expect Merleau-Ponty to accept this official version of Marxism. So what could it mean to say that he was a Marxist? To answer this question, we need first to go back to Merleau-Ponty's notion of human beings as essentially embodied subjects. Both the words in this phrase are important, individually and in combination. Human beings are subjects, but the particular form which their subjectivity takes is conditioned by the fact that they are embodied. Human beings are embodied, but the nature of their embodiment is conditioned by the fact that they are subjects. Our embodiment gives us roots in the material world: we are not some kind of timeless Reason, contemplating the world without reference to any particular time or place, but living beings who necessarily perceive the world from somewhere and at some time, and whose rational understanding is limited by this situation. Furthermore, this perception is not a mere contemplation of the world, but an interaction with it: the world is not something we simply observe in a detached way, but the place where we live.

This is a 'materialist' view of human beings, in the sense that it treats the human mind as inseparably connected to material conditions of existence, and ultimately to the biological needs of humanity as living organisms. But it does not *reduce* human beings to biological organisms; if that term refers to mechanistic systems whose every movement can be adequately explained by the laws of physics and chemistry alone. Because we are also subjects, we can 'transcend' our biological needs: even our most basic needs, such as those for food and drink and for sexual fulfilment, are given particular form by the ways in which we think about them, in a language which we share with others. These ways of thinking are shaped by our cultural history: the ways in which we now think are the outcome of a certain cultural tradition which has developed through the reflections of people in the past and in the present. So Merleau-Ponty's view could be called, using a term often used as a description of Marxism, 'historical materialism'. This description of Marxism applies more to the earlier thought of Marx than to the later, 'objectivist', version to be found in Marx's later writings and especially in the interpretation of them by Lenin, Stalin and other Soviet theorists. It was the rediscovery of the earlier writings of Marx which motivated the kind of 'humanist' revisions of Marxism found in the works of Lukács and Kojéve which so inspired Merleau-Ponty and led him to see Marxism (of this kind) as a natural extension of his own thinking.

The remarks in Marx's 'Eighteenth Brumaire' which were mentioned earlier neatly summarize this kind of 'historical materialism'. First, they emphasize that it is *human beings* who make history: history is not some kind of metaphysical force ('History' with a capital 'H') which does things to people, but simply the record of the things which people themselves have done in response to the problems posed for them by their situation. But secondly, they make it clear that the things which people do are not independent of their concrete situation and their material needs. What we must do before we can do anything else is to meet the problems of staying alive and reproducing the species, so that human beings will continue to exist. There is a clear sense in which this is fundamental. Since we are social beings, we need to find some form of social organization which will enable us to solve the problems of meeting these fundamental biological requirements. But the ways which human beings have found to meet these needs have developed over time, becoming more complex and sophisticated (and giving human beings more control over their natural environment). Each change in the method of meeting human needs has required a change in the social organization involved. Thus, the problems which human beings face have changed historically: the choices which they have to make are limited by the nature of the problems they have to solve at any given time. But this does not restrict them to only one choice: there is always more than one realistic way of conceiving of a situation, and so more than one way of proposing to solve a problem (though maybe only one which could be regarded as genuinely 'progressive', in the sense of opening up fresh possibilities for human life).

Something like this could be regarded as a summary of what Merleau-Ponty meant by 'Marxism'. It is 'humanistic' in the sense that it treats human choice as central to the way in which history develops. Human beings are not regarded as the mere playthings of impersonal historical forces, but as actively deciding their own destiny. It is not 'humanist', however, if that means that it sees human beings as independent of any material conditions, standing outside time, space and history. On the contrary, we cannot extract ourselves from the historical process and look on it from the outside. Paradoxically, that is just what 'objectivists' do: thinking of Marxism as 'scientific socialism', discovering the laws of historical change, requires us to assume we can treat historical change as an objective fact, just like, for example, evolutionary change in Darwinian theory, unaffected by what human beings think or decide. If, as phenomenologists, we set aside such objectivist assumptions, we can see that historical change is, in its very nature, a change in human ways of behaving and organizing themselves, and must be responsive to the ways in which those human beings think of how they have behaved and organized themselves in the past.

In many ways, this kind of 'humanized' Marxism fulfils the same role in Merleau-Ponty's thinking about society and its problems as his revised version of Freudian psychoanalysis plays in regard to understanding individual behaviour. We can best see how it differs from 'objectivist' Marxism, and from non-Marxist theories of history, by considering one of Merleau-Ponty's own examples (one which has briefly been referred to already: see Merleau-Ponty 2002: 517ff.). This has to do with the Marxist idea of 'class-struggle' as the motive-power of history. According to an objectivist interpretation, we should see social class as objectively defined: whether we realize it or not, we are 'objectively' members of one particular social class, defined by the circumstances of our lives, especially our position in the economic structure of society. In modern society, for example, we are either members of the bourgeoisie, the class which owns the means of production and lives off the income generated by the sale of its products, or we are members of the proletariat, the class which works for the bourgeoisie in operating those means of production, and has nothing to sell but its labour. This objective class-membership will be seen as causally determining our actions: the bourgeoisie, for instance, will necessarily want to hold on to its economic power and to increase its own profits by driving down the costs of production, including the costs of labour. The proletariat will, equally necessarily, want to resist the attempt to make it work harder and harder for less and less, so that there will necessarily be conflict between the two classes (class-struggle). This will be as inevitable as when two physical objects, each propelled by a physical force, encounter each other. And just as in that case, the outcome of the conflict will be in principle predictable, given knowledge of the relative forces involved.

On the other hand, someone who was completely opposed to any such 'materialist' interpretation of history – who thought of human beings as motivated only by rational evaluation of their situation – might read this situation in a totally different way. This would be what Marxists would call an 'idealist' interpretation of history, since it sees history as the outcome of disembodied ideas. On this view, what would determine a person's conception of their social position and values would be the arguments which convinced them, quite independently of what their material circumstances were. Someone, for example, could well decide to be 'classless', motivated by a humanitarian philosophy rather than by the economic interests of the class to which he or she objectively belonged. A businessman could try to run his business as a kind of community in which he and his employees were all treated as equals, and the maintenance of that community was regarded as more important than the maximization of profits. An objectivist Marxist need not deny that these things occasionally happened in history, but would nevertheless say that such 'top-down' attempts to create this kind of community could not result in genuine 'socialism' unless the bourgeois system was overthrown altogether. As long as this remained a capitalist business, the employer's efforts could at best lead only to a rather paternalistic system, in which the employees would not be truly equal to the employer, but would, like pet animals, be 'looked after' by the employer in order to work harder in the employer's interests. As soon as this kind of paternalism ceased to further these interests, the Marxist would say, the employer would revert more obviously to type, and the class struggle would be revealed in all its naked ugliness.

The objectivist Marxist thus denies that ideas have any real role in the social process, apart from their function in hiding the social realities from those involved. The idealist, on the other hand, gives them an independent part in deciding how society moves, as if material conditions were at most of subordinate importance. Each of the two opposing positions thus denies one half of Merleau-Ponty's conception of human beings as 'body-subjects'. Merleau-Ponty's interpretation of Marxism must obviously be different from either: it must give ideas some part to play while not making them entirely independent 'forces' in their own right. Both the objectivist and the idealist, to use a phrase which has been mentioned in a previous chapter, is guilty, each in their own way, of 'causal thinking'. That is, they try to understand the 'movement' of society as if it were like the literal movement of things through space, to be explained by causal laws of the kind familiar from classical physics. The difference between them is then that the idealist admits ideas as non-physical 'forces', which nevertheless behave like physical ones. But ideas cannot, Merleau-Ponty would say, be seen as determining action in the way that someone sitting on a see-saw and so putting pressure on that side of it determines the movement of the see-saw. An idea of, say, universal respect for all human beings can explain someone's actions only in that it provides a reason for acting in that way. The reason will influence the action only if the surrounding conditions make it possible to do so. Someone who employs other people in a business which can only survive if it makes a profit, however sincere his belief in universal respect for human beings, will not be able to put his ideas into practice without ceasing to be in business, and working instead for an overall change in the social system which will make possible respect of each human being for every other human being. There is nothing, in other words, to stop a person who starts off as a member of the bourgeoisie coming to side with socialism, but he can do so only if he ceases to be objectively a member of the bourgeoisie. (In the same way, of course, someone who starts off as a member of the proletariat could come to be a defender of capitalism.)

This implies that the objective conditions in which we find ourselves do not *determine* our ideas. There is no reason why a bourgeois could not come to see capitalism as unjust, or a proletarian could not be convinced by the arguments for free-market capitalism as increasing the general wealth of all. It cannot even be guaranteed that *all* or at least *most* members of the proletariat might not come to support capitalism, as seems to have happened in most advanced western societies. So no-one can predict, as the 'scientific socialists' sought to do, that a socialist revolution is inevitable. Whether or not socialism is a better system than capitalism must ultimately be decided, anyway, by moral argument, rather than by simple calculations of 'social forces', or by relying on the 'irresistible movement of History'. For that reason, Merleau-Ponty increasingly favoured, the more he thought about social change, some kind of liberal parliamentary democracy, which at least 'guarantees a minimum of opposition and truth' (1973a: 226). In a parliamentary system, for all its faults, those who held power were accountable ultimately to the electorate, and so could not become absolute masters of the state. Such a system therefore did not give preference to one person's or group's ideas over others, but allowed them to be subjected to rational criticism, the only sure way, given human limitations, in which truth could be arrived at. This is the – perfectly honourable – sense in which Merleau-Ponty's philosophy is 'humanist': his central concepts of embodied subjectivity and being-in-the-world allow him to give an account of the human situation as one of struggling to do what is best while lacking any absolute guarantee of what the 'best' might be.

CHAPTER 8

ART AND PERCEPTION

ART, TRUTH AND REASON

Phenomenology, in Merleau-Ponty's interpretation of it, is a philosophical method. Its aim is to put out of action the assumptions we normally make about ourselves and the world for scientific and practical purposes, and to get back to the world as we directly experience it in pre-reflective perception. At the beginning of the first of his 1948 radio talks, Merleau-Ponty says that 'laying bare' the world of perception in this way has been an achievement, not only of 'modern philosophy' (i.e. phenomenology), but also of 'modern art' (see Merleau-Ponty 2004: 39). By the term 'modern', as he goes on to explain, he means the philosophy and art of the preceding fifty to seventy years. As examples of 'modern art' in this sense he cites the names of Cézanne, Juan Gris, Braque and Picasso. These painters, and others like them, are seen by him as doing the same kind of job as the phenomenologist, though in a different, and perhaps even more effective, form. By examining what Merleau-Ponty has to say about them, which is interesting enough in its own right, we should be able to see better what he means by 'perception' and 'phenomenology'.

The examples given are all drawn from the visual arts, and much of what Merleau-Ponty has to say applies most obviously to that case. But he also wants to say similar things about the other arts – cinema, music, poetry and prose literature. We shall return to the other arts in the next section. In this section we shall concentrate on the visual arts, since his discussion of them contains the core of what he wants to say about art and its relation to philosophy. It is, as said in the last paragraph, specifically *modern* painting that Merleau-Ponty has in mind, the painting of the very end of the nineteenth century and the first half of the twentieth. Many people, faced with the works of the painters listed, complain that they do not represent what we actually see in the world. We are talking here, not about purely *abstract* paintings, which do not claim to represent what we actually perceive, but about paintings of people, fields, animals, houses, barges and so on (one criticism of Merleau-Ponty might indeed be that he does not really address the issues which arise in purely abstract painting). Classical painting is seen as presenting a much more 'realistic' view of things. It presents things in perspective, that great discovery of Renaissance painting: objects have firm outlines and definite colours, the colours that things 'naturally' have – snow is white, grass is green, and so on; things are arranged in space as we would normally expect them to be, and so on. In modern art, by contrast, perspective is often ignored, things have blurred outlines and colours that differ from 'what they should be', and the shapes and arrangements of things may seem to us to be distorted. How then can we say that modern art uncovers 'the world of perception'?

The first thing that must be said is that any work of art is, as such, a *creation* of the artist, not a mere reflection of some pre-existing reality. A painter, whether classical or modern, produces a work by putting paint on canvas. 'Painting', Merleau-Ponty says, 'does not imitate the world but is a world of its own' (2004: 96). This applies as much to classical as to modern painting. It applies even to photography, at least if a photograph is to be considered as a work of art. The photographer does not simply place the camera in front of a scene and allow the light coming through the lens to record what is before it. Rather, the angle and distance from which the photograph is taken is chosen, the picture is composed in the view-finder, and further 'interference with nature' may take place during the processing. The hand of the artist is even more obviously at work in painting of any kind. And we, the viewers, in so far as we are considering the work *aesthetically*, are, as Merleau-Ponty says, not concerned with whether it is a 'resemblance' of what it purports to depict, but with whether the world created by the artist is coherent, satisfying, illuminating, appealing and so on.

What we call 'realism' in painting, then, is not a matter of creating a resemblance of what we think we see in nature, but of a certain manner of constituting the world of the painting itself. In classical painting, by and large, this meant constituting the world of the painting in accordance with the requirements of what Merleau-Ponty calls 'knowledge and social living' (2004: 93). Living together with people in society requires us to be able to communicate with each other, and so to have *shared* conceptions of things and of the world in general. These shared conceptions are embodied in our language, and in the dictionary definitions of the words which we use. For example (Merleau-Ponty's own), the word 'table' can be defined as 'a horizontal flat surface supported by three or four legs, which can be used for eating off, reading a book on, and so forth' (Merleau-Ponty 2004: 94). Such a definition is held to express the 'essence' of the table, in the sense of what anyone must mean by the word, if it is being used intelligibly. The definitional meaning is thus the same for everyone. It is independent of any relation to any individual's subjective experience of any particular table, and in that sense is 'impersonal'. When we come to pursue theoretical knowledge or science, we idealize that impersonality further, treating our concepts of things as being independent of human experience altogether, as expressing the *objective* (in that sense) essence of the things: their reality as it is in itself.

Similarly with classical perspective. In the last essay which he published before his death, 'Eye and Mind', Merleau-Ponty considers this conception of perspective, as expounded by Descartes in his work *Dioptrics* (1964a: 171ff.). This is essentially a *geometrical* perception, expressed in terms of lines radiating from a point, as we might represent the relation of a camera lens to the objects in front of it. The camera lens is not a 'subject', a person with a point of view of his or her own, which would give the objects seen a particular meaning. The camera lens's relation to the objects in front of it is purely external or geometrical: it can be defined in terms of the straight lines between the objects and the lens. In this way, it is like the relation depicted in scientific optics between the human eye and the objects which affect the retina. Significantly, as Merleau-Ponty points out, Descartes takes line drawings as his typical examples of 'pictures': they lack colour, which, for Descartes, was no part of the 'essence' of a material object, but was simply the outcome of its relation to us as subjects. Painting or drawing, according to Descartes, is 'only an artifice which presents to our eyes a projection similar to that which the things themselves in ordinary perception would and do inscribe in our eyes' (Merleau-Ponty 1964a: 172). So once again painting is treated as an *impersonal* representation of the world as described by an objectivist science.

Modern art, by contrast, seeks, according to Merleau-Ponty, to get away from this conception of 'realism', in which 'reality' is what is expressed using the conventional concepts of ordinary social living and science, and art's main function is to 'represent' as accurately as possible the world as it would be perceived 'from nowhere'. Truth, in art as elsewhere, consists on this 'realist' view in accurate representation of a pre-existing 'reality'. Art, however, in Merleau-Ponty's view, is 'the act of bringing truth into being' (2002: xxiii). The classical artist, as much as the modern artist, does not merely reflect a reality which exists independently of human perception; rather, he or she creates a world which conforms to a conception created by human beings to meet the needs of science and social living. But, although we necessarily have these needs, the concepts which we construct in order to satisfy them get their meaning from our more basic, pre-reflective and personal contacts with the world around us. Modern art goes back to 'perception' in that more basic sense, in which it is 'defined as access to truth' (Merleau-Ponty 2002: xviii), because it is our contact with the world in *living* it, rather than thinking about it. In this way, modern art can be seen as 'realist' in a more fundamental sense: it reveals objects stripped of all the conceptual clothing in which we try to reduce them to instruments serving our own various purposes. In this sense, painting leads us back to 'a vision of things themselves' (Merleau-Ponty 2004: 93). The modern artist constructs a world, but seeks to do so in a way which remains faithful to phenomena, in the sense of objects as we actually perceive them, and out of which the meanings of our more sophisticated constructions arise.

Thus, Cézanne is said, by 'remaining faithful to the phenomena in his investigations of perspective', to have discovered that 'the lived perspective, that which we actually perceive, is not a geometric or photographic one' (Merleau-Ponty 1964b: 14). The relation between the various objects and planes depicted in a modern painting is a relation *in which they stand to a subject*, the painter or the person viewing the painting, not some kind of impersonal relationship to a point in the world, such as a human retina or the film in the back of a camera. The painter is trying to reveal a truth about the world as he or she lives it, a world experienced as meaningful for him or her. This truth is revealed by constructing on canvas a world which embodies those meanings. The subject does not merely represent objective truth: subject and object are inseparably intertwined. The work expresses a meaning which has its source in the artist's individual life (see

Merleau-Ponty 1964b: 19). For example, Cézanne appears to have had a rather withdrawn and alienated personality, which made it difficult for him to be involved in normal human relationships and society. This may explain, as Merleau-Ponty suggests, his remark that a human face should be painted as an object, and in general his tendency to depict the world in a detached and impersonal way. He thus liberates us from our usual tendencies to see the world in terms of its human usefulness or emotional associations, and depicts in his pictures the 'inhuman nature' to which human beings attribute utility or emotional force. Paradoxically, the meaning of the world which he creates in his pictures is its very lack of, at any rate certain kinds of, meaning. But of course, Cézanne's, or anyone else's paintings, only count as 'works of art' to the extent that others value them. The artist's skill lies in embodying a vision derived from his or her own experience in a way which will 'make their idea take root in the consciousness of others' (Merleau-Ponty 1964b: 19).

Painting thus communicates one individual's subjective experience to others, without embodying it in any impersonally intelligible form. How is this possible? We can go some way towards answering this question if we consider some of Merleau-Ponty's reflections on language. If we think first of the ordinary language which we use in everyday conversation, and, in a much more refined and precise form, in the discourse of science, then we can see it as *rule-governed*. We use expressions in accordance with rules which both speaker and hearer understand, and which say when it is correct to use a term and when it is not. (This is the point of the dictionary definitions referred to earlier.) So, if we are both English-speakers, and standing by a table, then I can understand your statement, 'This table is too small for all my papers to go on it' without any difficulty at all – at least as long as you are using terms in accordance with the rules. The words used *mean the same* for both of us, because their meaning is not tied to your, or my, associations with the expression, but to impersonal rules accepted equally by all English-speakers. If there is any danger of our 'talking at cross purposes', then it can normally be corrected as soon as it is discovered, by the simple expedient of agreeing on the rules which we both follow.

This can be widened, to include rationality in general. If I ask someone, 'Why are you running down the road so quickly?' and he replies, 'Because I'm in a desperate hurry to catch the last collection at the letter-box', then I would normally regard that as a sensible answer. The other person's behaviour would be rationally intelligible, because the reasons for it conformed to some rules or norms which both he and I (and millions of others) accept. But if he answered, 'Because the fairies are dancing in my primrose patch', then, in default of any further explanation of what he meant, I should find his answer baffling and irrational. It would not conform to the shared norms which constitute rationality. Shared rules of language and rationality are in this way essential to living together in a society and communicating with each other. 'Reason' and 'truth', in this sense, are regarded as already constituted, independent of the wishes or feelings of any individual, and in this way *impersonal*. We are born into an already existing language and already existing criteria of rationality, just as we are born into an existing society and culture – indeed, a culture is constituted in large part by its language and shared norms of rationality.

But language is something which is used by people to convey meaning; and the norms of rationality emerge from discussion between people: in this sense, both language and rationality are ultimately rooted in personal experience. Language can for this reason be used creatively – bending the rules in order to convey some *new* meaning, beyond that contained in the conventional rules. This will express a new way of looking at the world, and so the possibility of extending the concept of what is rational. The visual arts, at least in their modern development, are not a 'language' in the conventional sense: they do not express meaning by means of generally accepted rules. But they can nevertheless express meaning in a more basic way: this meaning will be a *new* one, a new way of looking at the world and the objects in it, which is originally peculiar to the artist, but which he or she manages to 'awaken' by his or her skill in at least some of those who look at his or her work. This is why a mere rational analysis of a painting, in terms of existing norms of rationality, will never be able to replace a direct *experience* of the work itself (see Merleau-Ponty 2004: 95). A primary role of the arts in general, in Merleau-Ponty's view, is to expand the concepts of rationality of conventional society, to lead people to look at the world afresh (see Merleau-Ponty 1964b: 19).

THE OTHER ARTS

The discussion so far has concentrated more or less entirely on the visual arts, because Merleau-Ponty's remarks on them illustrate most clearly what he has to say about art in general, and because we tend to take the sense of sight as our model when thinking about perception. But it is worthwhile seeing how far Merleau-Ponty's remarks about the modern visual arts can be extended to the other arts, if we make proper allowance for relevant differences. 'Perception', for him, is certainly not confined to visual perception, but applies to all pre-reflective contact with the world. One of our other senses, for example, is *hearing*, and that is the sense, obviously, which is most relevant to the art of music. Like painting, a piece of music does not *refer* to the world or to objects: it exists as a 'world' in its own right, one created by the composer. Even programme music, which Merleau-Ponty talks of as if it were a possible exception, is not really so. If we consider Beethoven's 'Pastoral Symphony', for instance, whose movements are labelled as scenes from country life, we surely cannot properly describe the music as *referring* to these scenes, in the way in which, say, a literal prose description would, or indeed as the titles of the parts of the work do. The music may *evoke* storms or peasant merry-making, but it does not *describe* them. We have not learned anything new about these things after listening to the music, and we appreciate the symphony because of the pleasure given by its evocations, rather than because we recognize the truth of its descriptions. In this way, programme music is no different from any other kind of musical work. It is a succession of sounds which in some mysterious way, not governed by any rules like a conventional language, cohere with each other to constitute a world. This world, as Merleau-Ponty says, 'exists in the universe of possible music' (2004: 99). I do not appreciate it, as he goes on to say, by *reflecting* on it, thinking about the memories which it may lead me to recall, or about the composer and his or her life, or even about the emotions which it may inspire in me. Rather, I just *listen* to it, and so enter into the world created by the composer, in the same way that I listen to sounds in nature and so enter into that world. Unlike the world of nature, of course, this is a world which is *just* made up of sound, and which, moreover, has a meaning which flows from the personal experience of the composer. If the composer's skill has created a sound-object which conveys that meaning to me, then the meaning is inseparable from the way in which it is expressed, and cannot be conveyed in words. This therefore does not seem to be like the way in which visual art can lead us to see the existing world in a new light.

The literary arts seem at first sight to be different from both visual art and music. By definition, their medium is language; and that language, apart from special cases like nonsense poetry, is a language in the ordinary sense. Poets, novelists and short-story writers write in English, or French, or Russian, just like journalists or the authors of scientific papers. The words they use thus have a conventional reference to objects and situations. When a novelist, for example, talks about 'the table in the dining-room', her words mean the same as they do when used by an estate-agent or a furniture salesman. But literature is not a description of the 'real world': this is most obviously true of poetry, but it is equally clearly the case with prose fiction.

Two examples may make the point clearer. First, one from poetry. When the American poet e. e. cummings created the following line in one of his poems: 'nobody, not even the rain, has such small hands', he was not making a statement about the size of someone's hands. It would obviously be inappropriate either to ask who he is talking about, and whether it was in fact true that she had small hands. And to say that the rain has hands at all, let alone small hands, would, in any normal prosaic context, be meaningless. A second example is taken from a novel, Ian McEwan's *The Comfort of Strangers*. The novel concerns two English people, Mary and Colin, who are on holiday in Venice. By chance, one evening they meet a stranger called Robert, who takes them through the city, and thereafter has a profound effect on their lives. Again, Ian McEwan is not narrating an account of what actually happened to three people called Colin, Mary and Robert. Whether or not the originals of these three characters really exist or existed, and whether or not what he says happened to them is factually correct, is clearly irrelevant. In both the two examples, words which have a meaning in the English language, and which are conventionally used to make true statements of fact about real people, places and things, are being used to create a world distinct from the world of real people, places and things. The words used here get their meaning, and certainly their reference, within the context of this created world, of the poem or the novel.

This may seem at first sight to be wrong. It might be possible to accept as true that the *reference* of an expression is to something or someone within the world of the poem or novel: the statements about Robert, Mary and Colin clearly refer to the characters in the novel, not to any real person, living or dead. Even when a historical character is referred to in a novel, as Napoleon is in Tolstoy's *War and*

Peace, it would seem inappropriate to cite historical evidence to 'disprove' any statements made about him there. *In the novel*, Napoleon figures as participating in its fictional world, not in the historical sphere. But does this apply to *meaning*? When e. e. cummings talks about 'rain' or 'hands', he surely means by those terms what we normally mean in English: if he didn't, then we couldn't even begin to understand his poem as anything more than 'music', a set of meaningless sounds. And when Ian McEwan, for instance, talks of Mary as 'brushing her hair', he surely means what we all mean by 'brushing' and 'hair'. If he didn't use words in their standard senses, then he could not fulfil what is surely one of the primary functions of the novelist, namely, to tell a story. Of course, sometimes in literature, especially in poetry, the standard meaning of words is *extended* in new and interesting ways. In his posthumously published work, *The Prose of the World*, Merleau-Ponty cites the case of the French novelist Stendhal, who extended the ordinary meaning of the French word which we could translate as 'rogue' by applying it to a character in one of his novels who did not quite fit the ordinary meaning of the word. In so doing, Stendhal caused his readers to see 'roguishness' in a new way – much as a painter leads us to see the pipe which he paints in a new light (see Merleau-Ponty 1973b: 12).

Generally, however, what Merleau-Ponty seems to be getting at in his discussions of literature is something other than this kind of extension of the meaning of ordinary words. It is rather the way in which ordinary words may be used to create parallel worlds which lead us to see the world in which we live differently. Cummings's talk of 'the rain' as having 'small hands', and his comparison of the small-handed woman to whom his poem seems to be addressed to the rain, leads us to a new imaginative understanding of love. And in another way, the characters and the place which Ian McEwan creates, again using words in their standard senses, embody his personal way of seeing people and communicate that different mode of seeing to his readers. But just because writers *do* use words, with their standard meanings, to create their worlds, there seems to be a difference between the way in which a poem or novel help us to see the world in a new light and the way in which a painting does. Their verbalism allows them to be more reflective, particularly about our relations with other human beings: in this way, they have an essentially *moral* dimension which is lacking from purely visual art, or from music. (Ian McEwan's novel referred to above, for instance, is said by some critics to convey the 'power of evil'.) In this sense, Merleau-Ponty's attempts to give the same treatment to all the arts seem to break down.

Finally, we can consider another art which Merleau-Ponty discusses in several places, namely, the cinema. The cinema is, in an important sense, a visual art; but it is also a *narrative* art, like a novel: the visual images are used to tell a story. In his 1948 radio lectures, Merleau-Ponty is a little disparaging about cinema up to his own time. He says that, 'Cinema has yet to provide us with many films that are works of art from start to finish' (Merleau-Ponty 2004: 97). This seems an amazing thing to say in 1948, given the great cinematic works of the likes of Eisenstein, Griffith, Jean Renoir, Abel Gance, Fritz Lang, John Ford, Orson Welles, and many others which had appeared before that year. But Merleau-Ponty, as he goes on to explain, is talking mainly about the commercial Hollywood cinema, the 'dream factory' which mass-produced escapist films of a greater or lesser degree of sophistication. Even these films are disparaged by him, not because they fail to be works of art at all, but because they are not such works 'from start to finish': and that is because he claims that, in their quest for commercial success, they 'eschew properly cinematic means of expression' ibid.).

What are these cinematic means of expression? Merleau-Ponty mentions on the next page such things as 'the selection of episodes to be represented', 'the choice of shots', 'the length of time allotted' [to them], 'the order in which they are to be presented' and 'the sound or words with which they are or are not to be accompanied' (Merleau-Ponty 2004: 98). These factors together will form a 'cinematographical rhythm'. So, what makes a film truly 'cinematic' is not so much the story to be told in it, which, as Merleau-Ponty says, could be told in some other form; it is rather the *way* in which the story is told. Perhaps at some time in the future, he suggests, when we have accumulated sufficient examples of truly cinematic films in this sense, then we shall be able to create a 'rule-book' of cinematic art. This will amount to a 'logic, grammar, or stylistics' of the cinema which we can use to decide whether in any particular case the proper weight has been given to each of the elements mentioned.

This idea of a rule-governed art of the cinema, however, seems to be inconsistent with Merleau-Ponty's remarks about the other arts. It seems to imply that cinema has a 'language' in the standard sense, of a means of communication subject to rules. But if so then cinema surely ceases to be a truly creative activity, enabling us to look at the world afresh, without the mediation of the conventional concepts embodied in language. Merleau-Ponty himself seems to recognize this, and to backtrack immediately. The 'rule-book' he speaks of would, he goes on to say, just be a matter of making explicit the relationships between elements which we are implicitly aware of in existing works. Creative film-makers in the future would still have to 'discover new relationships without being guided to them', so that 'the way we experience works of cinema will be through perception' (Merleau-Ponty 2004: 99). If so, however, there seems little point in speaking of a 'rule-book' at all: cinema, like the other arts, can be taken to communicate in ways which are not governed by rules, but which involve instead constructing a world which will 'awake' in the viewers the film-maker's own vision of things.

Elsewhere, Merleau-Ponty speaks of the film as 'not a sum total of images but a temporal *gestalt*' (1964b: 54). The word *gestalt* here is derived from the '*Gestalt* psychology' already referred to in an earlier chapter, which emphasized that we perceive situations as structured wholes, rather than as collections of unrelated or 'atomistic' elements. In saying that a film is a 'temporal' *gestalt*, Merleau-Ponty is affirming that the development of the film over time constitutes such a structured whole. Our perception of it must therefore likewise be of a structured whole over time: we grasp the film as a narrative when we follow the rhythm of the shots which make it up, seeing the connections between different shots, and the way in which each carries the story of the film further. The 'meaning' of the film thus does not lie in some 'idea' which can be separated from this narrative, but is something which emerges from our perception of the narrative itself, and which cannot be expressed except in the narrative. In following the narrative, and the various human actions and relationships which it contains, as depicted in the film, we come to understand human behaviour more generally as having the same kind of temporal structure. In this way, Merleau-Ponty argues, films make clearer to us what is meant by 'being-in-the-world', and 'being-in-the-social-world' in particular.

ART AND PHILOSOPHY

At the beginning of this chapter, we mentioned the way in which Merleau-Ponty saw modern art and modern philosophy (that is, phenomenology) as fulfilling essentially the same role. Both amount to a reassertion of the claims of 'perception' over those of theoretical reflection as guides to truth. Now that we have considered art in general, and the various particular forms of art, we can perhaps begin to see more clearly what Merleau-Ponty means by 'perception' as a basis for philosophy; and this will be a good way to round off this book as a whole. The best place to begin is probably by thinking again about the way in which the arts communicate truth, and what kind of truth it must be to be communicated in this way. Apart from the brief aberration referred to just now, in which Merleau-Ponty appeared to suggest that there might be a 'rule-book' for cinema, in general his view seems to be that the arts communicate in ways which are independent of the ordinary rules of language. Those rules are essential for the purposes of ordinary social life and the pursuit of science, or knowledge. For these purposes, we must always use words and expressions in the same way, no matter who we are. 'Table', 'perception', 'atom', 'gene' and so on must mean the same for you as they do for me, if conversation and discussion between us are to be possible, and if we are to arrive at truths which are the same for both of us. If we both, for example, mean the same by all the expressions in the sentence, 'This table is 2 metres long and a metre wide', then we can agree on how we should try to see whether it is true or false. Its truth or falsity is, as it were, there already, waiting for us to discover it. In ordinary social life, and even more in the sciences, we require such already-constituted and so discoverable truth: if we had no way acceptable to everyone of deciding on the true dimensions of tables or other items of furniture, for instance, then we could not engage in the buying and selling of furniture, or in the craft of furniture making, or in the scientific study of such objects.

The arts, however, according to Merleau-Ponty communicate without rules: the artist conveys to his or her audience a personal vision of things, not by describing that vision in rule-governed language, but by creating something which embodies the vision and which can awaken the same experience in those who are willing and able to respond to it. The truth communicated in this way is not something which exists already, waiting to be discovered, but something which is inseparable from the means by which it is communicated – the work of art. In this sense, the artist 'brings truth into being'. Furthermore, it is not available to everyone in the way already-constituted truth is. Anyone who knows what the expressions 'table', '2 metres long' and so on mean, can decide on the truth of the statement, 'This table is 2 metres long'. But only someone who is willing to open himself or herself up to a particular work of art can grasp its truth.

The rule-governed language in which we make statements in science and social life thus conveys an accepted view of what the world of things and of people is like. The artist, however, has a vision of the world which deviates from that generally accepted view. If it is too idiosyncratic, or if the artist lacks the skill to embody the vision adequately in the works which he or she creates, then clearly that vision will not be communicated to anyone else. But if an artist has a new vision of things or people which can be communicated to large numbers of people, then the artist will be able to change the ways of seeing of at least those people. What the artist has to 'say' (in whatever form of 'saying'), as Merleau-Ponty puts it, 'summons one away from the already constituted reason in which "cultured men" are content to shut themselves, towards a reason which contains its own origins' (1964b: 19). In refreshing the perception of the world, the artist is thus also extending the idea of what is 'reasonable'.

But we can always ask, of course, whether this is legitimate. After all, the people we call 'mentally disturbed' also have a personal vision of the world which differs in important ways from the one in which 'cultured men' shut themselves: we do not call this an extension of the idea of what is reasonable, but something which is entirely *un*reasonable. Is the artist just a mentally disturbed person? One important difference is that the artistic vision is one which is capable of shifting the perceptions of 'cultured men', in a way which the view of the world which we call 'mentally disturbed' is not. The artistic vision seems to draw on something which most human beings have in common, even if it is not something which human beings have formalized in the rules of a conventional language. And this might be reinforced by thinking about some things which have already been said about language. The words of conventional language get their meaning from human experience: to take a very simple example, the word 'table' gets its meaning from people's experiences of tables. But each individual's experience of tables is different, and indeed any individual will experience tables in different ways at different times: at different angles, from different distances, in different contexts, with different cultural associations, and so on. The word applies equally to tables of different shapes and sizes and designs and made of different materials. The rule which determines the shared meaning of the word 'table' abstracts from all these individual differences and focuses only on those aspects on which people have to agree if the purposes of social living and knowledge are to be achieved. In this sense, the conventional meaning of the word is an *abstraction* from the varieties of individual experience.

The artist, whether painter, poet, novelist or film-maker, can however make us aware of aspects of our subjective experience of even such a simple object as a table which escape our notice if we are preoccupied with the purposes of social living and knowledge. Merleau-Ponty speaks of the way in which modern painters like Cézanne can present us in their work with simple objects like lemons, bunches of grapes, or tobacco-pouches 'that do not pass quickly before our eyes in the guise of objects we "know well"' (2004: 93). Instead, as presented in their work, these familiar objects pose questions about our ordinary experience of them, and make us look at them, and at the world, afresh. We are forced to go back behind the comfortable set of concepts which we have constructed out of our direct experience and to return to the direct experience itself. The visions of someone who is mentally disturbed may be equally disconcerting, but in a different way from the artist's vision. The artist forces us to *extend* our sense of the possible meanings we can find in our experience: that is, to become aware that there are ways of being 'reasonable' other than those which we conventionally recognize as such in our social life.

This sheds light on what Merleau-Ponty sees as the function of phenomenological philosophy, and why he sees modern art as having in some ways a similar function. The main western philosophical tradition has seen philosophy as linked with science and with scientific concepts of rationality. Sometimes, this has been taken to mean that philosophy is itself a kind of 'super-science', which constructs even more general and comprehensive explanations of the world and the things in it than those disciplines we normally call 'sciences' – physics, chemistry, biology and so on. Sometimes, in the empiricist and positivist traditions, the link of philosophy with science has been considered to be that philosophy is 'the logic of the sciences', that its job is simply to analyse the concepts of science and the logical relationships between, for instance, theories and the evidence on which they are based. In either case, it is taken for granted that the only worthwhile way of describing and explaining our experience is that of the sciences, above all the natural sciences. It is this assumption which Merleau-Ponty calls 'objectivism'.

The phenomenological philosopher, like the modern artist, recalls people to the world of *perception*, from which the objective world of science is a kind of abstraction. As Merleau-Ponty says at the beginning of the first of his 1948 radio talks, this statement of phenomenology's aims may sound surprising. After all, isn't the world of perception the familiar world, the world we know best of all? Merleau-Ponty describes this as a 'delusion'. As long as we view things through the spectacles of our practical and social needs, the world of perception remains hidden from us. The job of phenomenology is to take away these spectacles from us in order to let us look at things directly – to return, as Husserl had put it, 'to the things themselves'. But to look at the world afresh in this way is precisely what, according to Merleau-Ponty, modern art, literature, music and film enable us to do. So what, if anything, differentiates philosophy from art?

One obvious difference between phenomenology and at least the visual arts is that phenomenology uses *language*, in the sense of the rule-governed language which we also use in everyday social life and in science. Literature, of course, also uses language. We shall come back shortly to the differences between literature and philosophy, but for the moment let us concentrate on what they have in common. As we saw earlier in the chapter, the very fact that literature uses language as its medium allows it to be more *reflective* than the visual arts or music. In this respect, literature is a *philosophical* art in a way that painting is not. But the kind of philosophy that is found in most of literature is *phenomenological*: more traditional kinds of metaphysics, in which, as said earlier, philosophy is seen as a 'super-science', do not fit readily into literary form. At best, they may be expressed in such forms as Plato's dialogues, which are certainly imaginative and intriguing as literature, but in which the philosophy is dominant. In his essay 'Metaphysics and the Novel', Merleau-Ponty says, 'Everything changes when a phenomenological or existential philosophy assigns itself the task . . . of formulating an experience of the world, a contact with the world which precedes all thought *about* the world' (1964b: 27–28). If so, then it becomes possible to conceive of a work which integrates literature and philosophy, in which the literary and philosophical elements are indistinguishable from each other.

This only raises a further question, however. What, then, if anything, is the specific role of 'pure' philosophy, that is, of philosophy which is not expressed in literary or other artistic form? The arts, even literature, do not, after all, engage in *explicit* philosophical reflection. They don't *describe* our direct involvement with the world, but *present* us with it. As Merleau-Ponty says in *The Structure of Behaviour*, the arts raise our awareness of the way in which our individual experience 'inheres in' a wider world, of which we are just a part (see Merleau-Ponty 1965: 176). In making us aware, they present us with the material on which we can reflect. Phenomenological philosophy, on the other hand, seeks to *describe* our inherence in the world. It does so using the same language that is used in science; but it differs from science in that the latter offers an *explanation* of the way the world of immediate experience is – an explanation which we tend to confuse with a description of that world, which has greater claim to reality than our ordinary awareness itself.

This brings us to a fundamental problem with Merleau-Ponty's phenomenology, one which he himself recognized in the work which he left unfinished at his death, *The Visible and the Invisible* (1968). Describing immediate experience of the world, or the world as we immediately experience it, is not the same as *having* that experience. It involves stepping back from our actual inherence in the world in order to reflect on it. In this respect, it involves detachment from being-in-the-world almost as much as scientific explanation of experience does. Because it is expressed in the same kind of language as scientific explanation, it uses concepts which, although rooted in immediate experience, nevertheless transcend it in order to be intelligible to any language-user. Even to talk of 'inhering in' the world, for example, is to describe our relation to things *from the outside*, as it might look to an outside observer: it is not to be identified with actually inhering in things, as we experience it *from the inside*. Description in language, by its very nature, seems to require a distinction between the describer and what is described, between consciousness and its objects. Phenomenology thus seems to defeat its own aims. For this reason, in *The Visible and the Invisible*, Merleau-Ponty concludes that 'the problems posed in *Phenomenology of Perception* are insoluble because I start there from the "consciousness–object" distinction' (1968: 200).

His answer in that later work is to try to get away from phenomenology altogether and to present, in a more Heideggerian style, our bodily involvement with the world, in which ourselves and our world are not distinguished: he uses the notion of 'flesh' or 'carnal being', which he calls 'the concrete emblem of a general manner of being' (Merleau-Ponty 1968: 147). It is frustrating that, because of his death, Merleau-Ponty never succeeded in fully developing these ideas. Certainly, in their present form, they are hard to make much sense of, though other passages in his later writings seem to suggest that what he had in mind was perhaps the replacement of philosophy by a kind of anti-philosophy, or a replacement of philosophy as such by the arts. But if art can only present our inherence in reality, leaving us to reflect on it, then the question still arises of how we do reflect on it, except in the traditional philosophical style. Reflection on experience essentially involves detachment from direct involvement with the world. So we seem to be back where we started. Perhaps what all this suggests is that we should see phenomenology simply as a philosophy which re-instates the validity of our ordinary, pre-scientific, ways of conceiving of ourselves and the world, against the constant tendency in our culture to denigrate those ways. Certainly, most of Merleau-Ponty's own insights would fit with that way of thinking of his philosophy: so that this may be as good a way of ending this book as any.

BIBLIOGRAPHY

WORKS BY MERLEAU-PONTY CITED IN THE TEXT (IN CHRONOLOGICAL ORDER OF ENGLISH TRANSLATIONS)

Merleau-Ponty 1964a: *The Primacy of Perception and Other Essays*, ed. J.M. Edie; Evanston, Ill.: Northwestern University Press.

Merleau-Ponty 1964b: *Sense and Non-Sense*, trans. H.L. and P.A. Dreyfus; Evanston, Ill.: Northwestern University Press.

Merleau-Ponty 1965: *The Structure of Behaviour*, trans. A.L. Fisher; London: Methuen.

Merleau-Ponty 1968: *The Visible and the Invisible*, trans. A. Lingis; Evanston, Ill.: Northwestern University Press.

Merleau-Ponty 1973a: *Adventures of the Dialectic*, trans. J. Bien; Evanston, Ill.: Northwestern University Press.

Merleau-Ponty 1973b: *The Prose of the World*, trans. John O'Neill; Evanston, Ill.: Northwestern University Press.

Merleau-Ponty 2002: *Phenomenology of Perception*, trans. Colin Smith; London and New York: Routledge.

Merleau-Ponty 2003: *Nature: Course Notes from the Collège de France*, trans. Robert Vallier; Evanston, Ill.: Northwestern University Press.

Merleau-Ponty 2004: *The World of Perception*, trans. Oliver Davis; London and New York: Routledge.

OTHER WORKS BY MERLEAU-PONTY

Signs, trans. R.C. McCleary; Evanston, Ill.: Northwestern University Press, 1964.

Humanism and Terror. trans. John O'Neill; Boston: Beacon Press, 1985.

In Praise of Philosophy and Other Essays, trans. J. Wild, J. Edie and J. O'Neill; Evanston, Ill.: Northwestern University Press, 1988.

Texts and Dialogues on Philosophy, Politics and Culture, ed. H.J. Silverman and J. Barry Jnr.; Amherst, NY: Humanity Books, 1992.

BIBLIOGRAPHY

WORKS BY OTHER AUTHORS REFERRED TO IN THE TEXT

Ayer 1936: Ayer, A.J., *Language, Truth and Logic*, London: Victor Gollancz.

Heidegger 1962: Heidegger, Martin, *Being and Time*, trans. John Macquarrie and Edward Robinson; Oxford: Basil Blackwell.

Husserl 1970: Husserl, Edmund, *The Crisis of European Sciences and Transcendental Phenomenology. An Introduction to Phenomenological Philosophy*, trans. D. Carr; Evanton, Ill.: Northwestern University Press.

Locke 1975: Locke, John, *An Essay concerning Human Understanding*, ed. Peter H. Nidditch; Oxford: Clarendon Press.

Marx 1988: Marx, K., "The Eighteenth Brumaire of Louis Bonaparte", excerpts in *Marx: Selections*, ed. Allen H. Wood; London: Macmillan, pp. 122–133.

Sartre 1969: Sartre, J.-P., *Being and Nothingness*, trans. Hazel. E. Barnes; London: Routledge.

SOME SUGGESTIONS FOR FURTHER READING

Gary Gutting, *French Philosophy in the Twentieth Century*. Cambridge: Cambridge University Press, 2001.

Monika Langer, *Merleau-Ponty's Phenomenology of Perception: A Guide and Commentary*. Basingstoke: Macmillan, 1989.

Eric Matthews, *Twentieth Century French Philosophy*. Oxford: Oxford University Press, 1996.

Eric Matthews, *The Philosophy of Merleau-Ponty*. Chesham, Bucks.: Acumen Publishing Ltd, 2002.

Stephen Priest, *Merleau-Ponty*. London and New York: Routledge, 1988.

INDEX

INDEX